WINNING
HIGH SCHOOL
DEFENSIVE FOOTBALL

WINNING
HIGH SCHOOL
DEFENSIVE FOOTBALL

LEONARD J. JACOBOWITZ

PARKER PUBLISHING COMPANY, INC.
West Nyack, N. Y.

To my wife, Nancy, who, thank God, can differentiate between a split end and a flanker, and who devotedly raises our children while I try to guide others

WHY I DECIDED
TO WRITE THIS BOOK

My reason for undertaking this work is to put down on paper the concepts, theories, and workable, teachable techniques that I learned the hard way—by trial and error, and by the ultimate criterion, success.

This success can, I believe, be directly attributed to our defensive system, which has allowed our opponents an average of only four points a game over the last several years. This book shows the high school coach how he can build an equally win-conscious defense.

To win consistently on the high school level the coach must develop a tradition of defensive football. Offensive football, it seems to me, places too great an emphasis on the great athlete, and it is highly improbable that any team would have great athletes year after year.

Also, offensive football has a tendency to change from year to year. One particularly good athlete may force a change in an offensive style of attack in order to fulfill his greatest potential.

The secret of winning, then, is *not* to wait for a good offense and excellent athletes but to *teach* hard-hitting defensive football. This book shows how to teach winning high school defensive football; it shows, among many other things, how to sell defense and how to toughen ball players, how to improve hitting ability and develop pride in it, how to teach tackling for keeps, how to teach gang tackling, how to confuse your opponents' blocking rules without stunting, how to make your opponents make mistakes, how to coach for the big defensive play, how to teach pursuit, when to use a goal line defense, how to train your defensive signal caller, how to teach blocking punts, how to stop momentum from the opposition, how to select defensive personnel, how to scout for defensive football.

In short, I decided to write this book to give the high school football coach a proven guide to developing a total defensive system that will win consistently.

Len Jacobowitz

ACKNOWLEDGMENTS

I wish to acknowledge the contributions of the football staff of Northport High School, Tom DiNuovo, Bill Martin, Dick Willets, and Richard Kasso, whose many ideas and concepts are incorporated in this text, and whose hard work and dedication have helped to create a truly fine defensive atmosphere at Northport. I also wish to thank Ed Berg, Sy Rapp, and John Ryder for so much of my basic thinking on defensive football.

CONTENTS

11

     System (cont.)

     Left Defensive Halfback
     Right Defensive End
     Left Defensive Tackle
     Left Defensive Guard
     Right Defensive Halfback
     Right Defensive Tackle
     Right Defensive Guard

11   How to Get Your Team Ready Mentally for a Winning
     Defense • 157

     Play Each Game as if It Were a Season in Itself
     21 Hours to Kickoff
     Let Them Sweat at Home

12   How to Scout for Defensive Football • 165

     What Do We Want to Know from a Scouting Report
     How to Organize Your Scouting Program
     Individual Play Chart
     Tendency Chart
     Formation Chart
     The Kicking Game
     Personnel

13   How to Develop a Weight Training Program for a
     Winning Defense • 187

     Five Exercises for Our Program
     Workout Progress Chart

14   Eleven Ingredients for Winning on Defense • 197

     You Must Want to Win
     You Must Have Reasons for Winning
     You Must Sacrifice to Win
     Be Willing to Work Harder than Anyone Else
     Have a Set Plan
     Maintain Great Pressure
     Accept Nothing but Perfection
     Have All Athletes Work to Peak Performance

HOW TO WIN FOOTBALL GAMES BY GETTING MORE DONE IN LESS TIME ON DEFENSE

HOW MANY GAMES SHOULD THE
COACH WIN IN TEN YEARS?

When football coaches congregate, the topic most debated is what wins football games. Usually, the following requirements are agreed upon:

1. Good athletes
2. Good football program
3. Tradition and desire to win
4. Good coaching

All factors being relatively equal, each school would win its share of all the football games played. In a ten-year period with eight teams in a conference, each team should win one or perhaps two championships. Unfortunately, this is never the case. Generally, one, two, or three teams in the conference will dominate the win and loss records.

We feel over a ten-year period that there will be: two years of superior material, two years of inferior material, and six years of about average material.

When material is superior, and the football players are great athletes, there is little coaching involved. The program will normally carry itself. It is difficult to make this type of athlete lose football games. It is generally agreed that with a team of this nature, a good staff will do less coaching than with a poor football team. A great football team will perform better a little undercoached.

On the other hand, during the two years of inferior material most coaching staffs will drive the players into oblivion and will cause themselves mental anguish, when there is little that can be done except teach good, sound, football. That leaves the other six years, when the material will be about average in conference comparison. This six-year period is when coaching takes place. The coaching staff which can continue to place its teams at or near the top of the conference year after year with average material, is what makes the difference between winning and losing football teams.

It is not personnel, program, or desire to win that develops a winning football team; instead, we feel it is good, sound, strong coaching that wins year after year and develops personnel, program and desire in the process. The sooner that most coaches realize that it is the staff themselves that will win, the sooner they will start winning consistently. This can be proven over and over again by looking across the nation at the outstanding high school coaches in each state. The top coaches are always in the 70 to 90 percent win bracket, and we believe they will take this record with them to any new school and continue to produce topnotch football teams.

HOW THE SYSTEM OF MASS FOOTBALL CAN WIN FOR YOU

High school coaches will watch great college football teams, and marvel at the training, discipline and skill of the football players. There are so many individual skills that have to be learned to make a great football team. Offensively and defensively at each position there are many coaching points to be made. On a good college coaching staff, however, there are eight men, while on a fine high school coaching staff there are only three men on the varsity level. *But the game is the same.*

We believe that to turn out championship high school football teams, you must have players who can react to each different situation during the course of a football game with various and appropriate skills. We must teach the same exact skills as a college coaching staff, because the game is the same. But with personnel that is not as experienced, how can we expect to do this when we have just enough time to teach basic skills, basic beginnings, basic attitudes? We can't. We don't expect to.

We feel you can accomplish all these things by teaching a thought, an idea, a belief—mass football. What is mass football? Mass football is constant movement. It is a great desire on the part of every individual. It is an ability to do things that were not taught in practice. It is an instinct, a reaction. How do we teach these mental attitudes that will compensate for specific knowledge of skills and for experience? We do it by the following methods:

1. All teaching should be done in the classroom, not on the football field. The first 20 minutes of each practice session are spent in the classroom. There are three different classrooms with three different coaches and three different groups.
2. When on the practice field, no one must ever be permitted to stand in one spot. There must be constant motion for the duration of the practice time, usually an hour and 50 minutes. We have only one exception to this. This is on tackling drill which is covered in Chapter 2, page 33.
3. There should never be a line waiting to perform any drill. Use only seven-man sleds. Give away your two-man sled. Drills should be organized so that the players move from drill to drill at a sprint.
4. All drills should be planned with two-thirds of the group working, and the other third waiting to move in at the first stoppage.
5. All groups should perform each drill one time, with

the waiting group moving immediately into position as soon as they are finished. Therefore, no one would be standing around for more than four seconds.

6. Teach one on one blocking by having seven against seven, one time each.

7. No drill or teaching maneuver should last more than two minutes.

8. If a drill requires people standing around, eliminate it.

9. All drills should be based on a go-go principle. If a boy is waiting to move into a drill, he should be running in place, clapping his hands until he moves into the drill. At no time must he stand still.

10. Have all groups organized so that seven-man sled, air dummies and blocking dummies are placed in different areas of the field. Practice is organized so that each group will move from drill to drill with at least a 50-yard sprint between. Do not run two successive drills in the same spot.

11. When scrimmaging, the offense should come up to the line of scrimmage against the second string defense or the second 11 men. They should run their play and regroup in the huddle. The third team should be on the sideline calling their defensive signal. As soon as the play is terminated, they must run onto the field and fill in on the defense while the second team regroups on the side of the practice field and calls their defensive signal for the next play. In this way, 33 men are running every second play.

12. Do not scrimmage for perfection. Scrimmage for hitting and constant movement. Use your movies for correction and perfection.

13. Develop the idea that standing still is a sin.

14. Do everything in mass. Tackle in mass; run ballhandling with four backfields moving at one time; pass with three quarterbacks throwing to three different sets of receivers in different directions, all centered around one coach. Block in groups of seven on seven.

15. Every six minutes of practice time on the field, have a manager or assistant coach blow two loud whistles. The squad should be mentally prepared to run a 50-yard lap around an object on the field, and then move right back into the individual groups with which they were working. This happens every six minutes on the field, from the first to the last day of practice.

16. Develop a feeling of "esprit de corps," a pride in belonging to a great unit (*Chapter 11*).

17. Push the group into mass exhaustion. Fourteen men should not be physically tired; 33 should.

18. Eighty-five percent of all corrections should be made in the classroom at the next practice session. Little practice time should be allowed for corrections.

19. Use only the first string offense and defense for corrections. Second and third stringers should learn most of the corrections on their own, and should be corrected in the classroom. Do not waste time on the practice field. Compensate for mistakes with movement.

YOU MUST SELL DEFENSE

If you are going to sell defense and defense is to be your forte, you must sell it hard, and consistently. Good defense, aside from being sound mechanically, must have great pride, almost passion, behind it. It is something that comes from a deep devotion or from the belief that defense will win, and will win all the time. It is an intangible thing. When you have it all other teams know you have it, and when they play you, they know how difficult it will be to score.

The following is a list of things we do to sell defense:

1. Spend 50 percent to 60 percent of all our practice time on defense.

2. Tell our team every single day that we are a defensive football team.

3. Place on a bulletin board a chart of all graduates playing college ball, their college, and the position each plays on defense.
4. At all rallies, banquets or team introductions always introduce the players by their defensive positions such as defensive halfback, defensive linebacker, defensive right tackle, etc.
5. Have defensive tackling charts placed throughout the school (*Chapter 4*).
6. Have defensive awards and trophies presented at football banquets and sports award dinners.
7. Develop a fierce pride in the ability to hit with the helmet (*Chapter 2*).
8. Sell the players on the idea that offense is a great deal of fun, and everyone enjoys playing it. However, *defense* is what wins football games!
9. Place a sign on the entrance to the coach's office reading, "Teams who make goal line stands win championships!"
10. In all practice schedules have defensive drills, tackling, and defensive scrimmage come before any offensive practice or drills.
11. On any successful win, place the credit for the victory primarily on the defensive unit, and single out any individual defensive performances.
12. Make the team believe that the greatest single accomplishment they can achieve is to shut out another team.
13. Have a chart made of any and all shutouts for the past five years. It should be placed where it may be seen the year round.
14. Select a defensive insignia to be awarded at the completion of each game for outstanding defensive play. We like the skull and crossbones decal (*Chapter 4*).
15. Develop pride in thinking that only tough men can play defense, as explained on page 24.

16. Stop practice every time a player makes a great hit or tackle where you can hear the pads rattle, and recognize his efforts with a compliment such as: "Jones, you are going to be a great football player!"
17. Have all meetings of the team called defensive meetings, whether they be used for offense, kicking game or defense. All notices of meetings should be referred to as defensive meetings.
18. Make sure your captains are elected from the defensive unit.
19. Develop a defensively oriented coaching staff. Each member should take great personal offense if his particular unit should be the cause of a score by another team.
20. Brainwash your team with a fever for hitting (*Chapter 2*).
21. Place pictures around the school of great gang tackling.
22. Develop the feeling among the team that it is almost impossible to score on your defense, that the defense as a whole will never give up a score; but the weakness of an individual player may.
23. Develop a rapport with the team so that when a coaching staff member meets a player and asks him, "What wins football games?" his reply will be, "Defense wins football games, coach!"

TOUGHNESS CAN BE TAUGHT

Every great football team has physical toughness in its players. It is the way they block, the way they tackle, the manner in which they move from one play to the next. We feel this toughness may be taught in much the same way that a Marine drill instructor would teach his troops. You must develop a Spartan attitude to win consistently.

The following list shows some of the ways we feel we can teach this attitude of toughness:

1. Have the coaching staff be tough. They should be in top physical condition, able to block against their players.
2. Have absolute discipline at all times (*Chapter 3*).
3. Have constant motion on the practice field.
4. Be unreasonable. Never be satisfied.
5. Have competitive toughness drills, such as challenge drills where only the strong survive.
6. Explain each year that there will be 150 candidates out for football and only 35 will survive, or have the guts to stay with it!
7. Develop the feeling that the player who misses a practice session lets down the entire squad.
8. Injuries, bruises, and sprains should be considered weaknesses.
9. Players should have the feeling that an injury will lose them their job.
10. Develop such a pride in winning that the team is afraid to lose.
11. Demand fierce hitting (*Chapters 2 and 3*).
12. Compare football with war!
13. Have the pre-season conditioning so tough that you are actually trying to have players cut themselves. Tell your players that only the strong will survive as members of the varsity football team.
14. Sell the players on the idea that one of the greatest acomplishments they will ever achieve is being on the varsity football team.

YOU CAN'T WIN IF THEY DON'T HIT

If you are to win consistently, you must have two basic ingredients: (1) the ability to hit, and (2) the quickness to get into position to hit. A great compliment is paid to a team when it is said that "that team can really hit!" That's what we are looking for. We want an opposing team to know that ours will be a hitting team.

Hitting is generally characterized by pads rocking, by vicious jolts to ball carriers, by fierce blocking and tackling in the open field, and by savage blocking on the line of scrimmage. We believe most high school football teams have one, two, or possibly three boys with this ability to hit. However, when you come up against a team of 11 defensive ballplayers with this ability, you know you're in for a tough afternoon.

We want our ball players to feel that they can hit as hard as any high school team in the country. We want our players to take pride in the fact that we have placed a tackle on the All-Long Island Team for the past four years.

It is very difficult to teach a boy how to hit. In most cases a boy will have the ability, and its development will come with maturation and experience. We feel you can coach hitting to some degree by teaching it in mass. The following are some of the methods to develop hitting:

HOW TO IMPROVE THE HITTING ABILITY
OF YOUR TEAM

1. Develop a pride in the ability to hit.
2. Emphasize hitting with the helmet.
3. Build up strength in the neck muscles with weights and neck bridges.
4. Develop the attitude that those who can not hit will be "among the missing."
5. Develop the attitude that if you do not hit you will get hurt.
6. Develop the attitude that when we hit, we hit for keeps.
7. Break huddles, both offensively and defensively, with a clap of the hands and the word "hit" shouted.
8. On the practice field when individual groups move from area to area or from drill to drill, they should shout "hit-hit-hit" on every second step.
9. Build a tradition of hitting. Tell stories of past ballplayers who were great hitters.

WIN AND WIN NOW

Great football teams all have a burning desire to win, and this desire sends them into a ball game with at least a seven-point advantage. A winning attitude is contagious. It consists of morale, tradition, confidence, and it creates an atmosphere of its own. The more you win, the more it is felt around you. The feeling spreads through the school, to the faculty, into the community, down to the junior high school program, to the press, and to your opponents. It can snowball to where the football itself will bounce in your direction.

The interesting thing about a winning attitude is that it doesn't pass, or block, or tackle, or produce great open field runners. It is a prevailing spirit surrounding you, and can win for you consistently. If you do not have it, you must have terrific athletic talent to win.

THE BUILDING OF A WINNING ATTITUDE

1. Win all the time.
2. Have assistant coaches and ballplayers feel in their hearts that you are going to win, and win all the time. Carry this attitude with you all year.
3. Tell the team every day that they are going to win. It must be a passion with them. Let them hear it so often that it becomes part of them.
4. The word lose is non-existent. It must never be mentioned.
5. Tell the team each day that we win because we work harder than any other; then proceed to work harder!
6. Play up every bit of tradition that you have. If you don't have any, create some!
7. Be the hero that your team wants you to be.
8. Build and sell football in the high school and community.

9. Have schedules and posters made and placed throughout the school and community.
10. Have individual ballplayer pictures taken and give them to merchants to place in the windows of stores.
11. Talk football all year around.
12. Sell the school on the importance of football.
13. Explain to the team the reasons for winning (*Chapter 14*, page 198).
14. Allow each letterman to purchase a football jacket. It should become a cherished tradition.
15. Treat anyone who is not sold on football like the plague!
16. High school students want to belong. Develop a great pride in belonging to the varsity football team. Make it a status symbol.
17. Develop in your team a fear of losing.
18. Have a football room where the varsity players dress, and each has his own locker with his name on it. No one but the varsity is allowed in. It should be a room where they can congregate the year round and socialize.
19. Make football important, particularly to the team.
20. Have a Hall of Fame, where past records of individual accomplishments are recorded. Especially significant would be records of defensive players: most tackles of a single game, most tackles of the season, most interceptions, most fumbles recovered, etc.
21. Each victory should be treated with exaltation; any defeat, with total depression. Upon a defeat, suffering must occur. All defeats should be blamed on not paying the price.
22. Victory should be assumed at all times, with the exception of the day of a game—and then reassumed after kickoff.
23. Instill in the team the desire to put forth 101 percent on every play.
24. Each player must have the feeling that he must do

more than one job on every play. He must go from whistle to whistle.

25. A feeling of complete dedication must exist.

26. The good name of the football team should be treasured.

2

HOW TO TEACH
TACKLING FOR KEEPS

We believe that all solid defense revolves around the ability to tackle. If you do not tackle properly and savagely, then all theories of defense are worthless. All is in vain if ultimately, at the point of contact, the tackle is not made or the hit is not followed through. There is no reason to teach any other fundamental until each player possesses the ability to tackle, and tackle for keeps. Never lose sight of this. All defensive strategy will be wasted unless you have the ability to tackle for keeps. We also believe very strongly in gang tackling (covered in this chapter) and pursuit (*Chapter 4*). "Hit with your head!"

We teach tackling with only one drill. We do not believe in lead-up tackling drills or form tackling drills. We usually use our live tackling drill only about five times a year. This drill is the first contact drill we will use at the beginning of the football season. It is the only drill we use throughout the year where we will have players standing around. At all other times they are in constant motion. This drill is the one exception. This drill breeds the type of hitting and contact we want throughout the season. Thus, a great amount of importance and build-up is associated with it. This drill has become a tradition at Northport, and varsity football candidates have come to expect it and know it will be their first contact drill. It has received such a build-up from one team to another, year after year, that we may have as many as 100 people on hand to watch this drill at the beginning of the season.

This drill, we believe, is largely mental, but it typifies the attitudes, mental and physical toughness, and desire to win that we expect from our football teams.

The drill begins by lining up our two biggest and best-hitting football players opposite each other at eight yards' distance. The rest of the squad lines up behind them, so there are two lines facing one another eight yards apart. We throw a football to one of the players. While each player waits, we preface the drill with a speech to build up tension to a peak. Each time we use the drill we repeat these same thoughts even though they may have heard it 25 times over a three-year period.

PRIDE IN HITTING

It goes something like this: "Gentlemen, at Northport we take tremendous pride in hitting with the head. We have the reputation of being the hardest hitting team on Long Island. Any player who has put on a Northport helmet in competition has hit with it. We hit, gentlemen, with the helmet only. We do not believe in arm tackles, shoulder tackles, or leg tackles. We hit with the helmet. Anyone who can not hit with the hat, and bring about vicious impact on contact, cannot play football for Northport. Everytime you make a tackle, your opponent must be stopped as though he had hit a brick wall. He must never move one inch forward after contact. Those of you that can hit and hit with authority with the helmet will play football here!"

THE DRILL FOR TACKLING

1. Head coach will stand between the two lines and will throw the football to the side carrying the ball after each tackle.
2. Assistant coaches will take a knee on the opposite side watching the contact.
3. On the whistle, the coach will throw the ball to the

first man on one line.

4. As the ball is thrown, the tackler will head full speed at the ball carrier.
5. The ballcarrier will run straight at the tackler and run over him.
6. Just before the contact, the tackler will lower his head, aiming at the ballcarrier's crotch.
7. The ballcarrier will run right through the tackler and trample him back.

We are looking for helmet to helmet contact; for the crack of the pads as the helmet strikes. After each hit a comment is made by the coach. If the tackle was satisfactory, both boys are complimented. If the contact was not satisfactory, the boys are required to repeat the drill. If after three tries a boy has still not made a satisfactory contact, he is told to go to the side and think about it. After a while the player is called back to try again. Usually the other boys on the team will shout encouragement to the boy to motivate him. If he is still unsuccessful, he will be sent to the Junior Varsity.

We go through the entire squad in this manner one time only, making comments on each boy's tackle and ballcarrying turn, and on each hit. In doing this we are building up the tradition of Northport hitting. This is the only way we teach tackling—individually.

HOW TO TEACH GANG TACKLING

All great football teams have the ability to gang tackle, to hit in mass, to have six, seven, or eight men in on each tackle. They have the ability to surround the ballcarrier from all angles on the football field. Wherever the ball is, there will be defensive players in numbers surrounding it.

GANG TACKLING CAN GIVE YOU THE WINNING EDGE

Good gang tackling will punish ballcarriers. It will give the ballcarrier the feeling that there is no place to go. In many instances, it will make a ballcarrier panic. Good gang tackling causes fumbles and mistakes.

Effective teaching of gang tackling will insure excellent angles of pursuit, and without excellent pursuit you will never have a great defensive football team. With proper teaching of gang tackling you will insure constant motion on the field by the defensive team, and will eliminate any standing around.

Over the years we have spoken with many coaches and students of the game about gang tackling; how it is best taught, its advantages, and how a team acquires it. We have experimented with different ideas and theories, and have come up with only one satisfactory way of teaching it. This method is as follows:

After defensive groups have been working individually for approximately eight days (the period of time it takes us to put in our basic defenses), and our basic defense has been taught, including reaction drills, pursuit drills, and key reading, we will bring the team together for some live defensive work. One assistant coach is given a foreign team or a dummy team, and this team will line up in a regular straight-T formation. Plays will be outlined on 5 x 8 cards. These plays will be basic, straight running plays such as off-tackle, fullback up the middle, dive plays and sweeps to both sides. The assistant coach will quarterback this team. The first defensive team is called out. Both teams are instructed to play until they hear the sound of the whistle. At this stage of our practice, when we have only one basic defense, they will line up automatically in it. They will still form a huddle and break from it, but there is no signal called in the huddle.

YOU MUST HAVE LIVE SCRIMMAGE

Just before we begin the live scrimmage we explain to the defensive unit that we are looking for gang tackling. We want each defensive player, as soon as he reads his key and fulfills his responsibility, to get onto the pile, up to the point where he hears the whistle. The head coach is the only person to blow the whistle to stop the play. The foreign team will come out and run a play. The head coach will blow a delayed whistle. It should be blown about one second later than it normally would be blown in a game. When this occurs, all 11 men in the defensive unit should be on the pile on top of the ballcarrier. The head coach must now find anyone on the defensive unit not on the pile and viciously chew him out. He should be laced into unmercifully.

The offensive team again regroups; the defensive team huddles and lines up on the line of scrimmage. Another play is run, a delayed whistle is blown, and the same procedure follows. You will tell the defensive unit you do not care if they cannot see the ballcarrier. They are to find that pile and throw their bodies onto it. At this point, piling on should almost be encouraged. Anyone not reaching the pile after being reprimanded once, should be replaced from the defensive unit at this time.

After about the third play, we will stop the scrimmage and explain again the purpose of the defensive unit. We are looking for gang tackling—seven, eight and nine men on each tackle. We want great pursuit and great movement. We want no excuses: each player must be on the pile.

We continue the procedure on plays to each side of the line. We will run a dive play, fullback, off-tackle, and a sweep to the right and then to the left. On each play, emphasis will be only on mass piling. This emphasis must come completely from the whiplash of the head coach's tongue.

The entire scrimmage will generally consist of perhaps 12 tackles. But I cannot emphasize enough the drive by each defensive player to get to the point of attack and fling his body on the pile. He must fight to get to the action, through, over, and around offensive players.

This defensive scrimmage will be the first mass team defensive scrimmage of the season. As the season progresses toward the first game, we will slowly begin emphasizing that the players must stop their drive and contact at the whistle. The coach will quicken his whistle with the emphasis that piling on is illegal. The sole purpose of this type of scrimmage is to emphasize a great desire to get to the action.

This particular scrimmage will be tough on the offensive backs, usually second and third string backs. But, as we tell our team every day, "It's a tough game!"

The described method of teaching gang tackling is the only method we have found to be effective. Our defensive unit, year in and year out, is notoriously noted for gang tackling.

To teach and emphasize gang tackling you must keep accurate tackling charts. The charts should be placed throughout the school two days following a game. The charts must have individual tackles and part tackles, and must be cumulative throughout the season (pages 60 and 61). On each play of a game there should be one full tackle awarded and as many part tackles as possible. The players must understand that if they can get anywhere near the pile, they will be awarded a part tackle.

3

HOW TO ORGANIZE A WINNING HIGH SCHOOL DEFENSE

GIVE THEM THREE

Sound defensive football teams realize that they will rarely stop any offense completely. But it is generally acknowledged that you must slow down the offensive team. An easy touchdown must never be allowed, be it a long run touchdown, a long pass touchdown, a punt return or kick-off return touchdown, or an intercepted pass touchdown. We feel good high school teams will make a mistake once in approximately 11 plays. We also feel that poor high school teams will make a mistake once in approximately seven or eight plays. Therefore, we can do two things: (1) we can slow our opponents down until they do make the mistake, or (2) we can create a mistake by fierce hitting!

In high school football, the mistakes will result from one of the following:

1. Missed assignment
2. Fumbles
3. Penalties
4. Pass interceptions
5. Center-quarterback exchange
6. Poor play call

We must slow down our opponents' offense, causing mistakes and possession of the ball or forcing them to punt. We impress upon the team that our opposition will make mistakes, and we cannot afford a defensive breakdown to permit the easy touchdown. As long as we do this, they will not score often if ever.

We want our defensive team to think in terms of allowing the offensive team three yards on each play. We play our defensive guards three to four feet off the line of scrimmage. This is to allow them to move laterally and be in a position to gang tackle whenever the ballcarrier comes across the line of scrimmage. We are willing to give the offense up to three yards on each play, but no more (*see Chapter 5*). We emphasize the fact that to give up a first down occasionally is reasonable. First downs do not appear on the scoreboard.

We seldom, if ever, go into a goal line defense on third down and short yardage. We sell the idea that the promised land is the goal line, and the remainder of the field is used primarily to entertain the spectators (*Chapter 9*—The Importance of Field Position, page 145). Each player must understand the theory completely that we are slowing down the other team's offense, not trying to stop them completely. Hence, our objectives are:

1. Slow down the offense.
2. Move laterally to be in a position to tackle (*Chapter 4*).
3. Allow them three yards and then punish the ballcarrier.

DON'T CHEAT ON THE DEFENSE

We believe you must not cheat on the defense to win consistently. We do not believe in monsters, or overshifting to the wide side of the field. We do not believe in stunts, trick defenses, slants or loops. We do not believe in red-dogging or blitzing, although on a rare occasion we may call a blitz. All of the mentioned techniques may win you an individual ball game, or may win for you a number of ball games. But they will not win for you year after year. We do believe that to win consistently you must teach players to beat their man. We want our football players to realize that we are not trying to fool anyone. We want them to understand that each one of them must individually whip his man. We believe we can teach this by employing the following:

1. In the off-season, develop an outstanding body, conditioning, and weight lifting program (*Chapter 13*). We want to build up our small boys, and trim down our heavy boys, to develop speed and strength to the best advantage. Our team should be the best-conditioned team in the conference.
2. Have our defensive system so uncomplicated that each player can master his position (page 51).
3. Keep each individual position as simple as possible so that individual guilt can be ascertained on a breakdown.
4. Each individual defensive position should be so well drilled that reaction becomes instinctively automatic (page 45, "Don't Make Mistakes").
5. Concentration should be on *hitting*, not on figuring out what to do.
6. Set up game situation drills.
7. Spend enough time practicing on defense so that each player feels secure in the knowledge that he will respond and react quickly without having to think. His only concern should be the man he is playing.
8. Develop great pride in each man; the feeling that he is the best; that when he is working to maximum capacity, no one can beat him.

We are trying to sell our team the conviction that we are not trying to trick anyone or fool anyone; that we will line up in our defense and bang like hell! We are trying to build pride in "Here we are, come beat us!"

CONFUSE THEIR BLOCKING RULES

One of the quickest ways to get an opponent to make mistakes is to confuse his blocking rules. A defensive team that can consistently keep the offense confused on blocking assignments will have gained the greater advantage. The more confusion, the sooner a mistake will result, and possession of the ball will change hands.

There are many ways to confuse blocking assignments. I have listed some of them as follows:

1. Stunting
2. Looping
3. Slanting
4. Shuttling
5. Blitzing
6. Changing defenses frequently
7. Confusing individual offensive linemen

Of all of the above, we believe in only numbers six and seven. The rest have a tendency to reduce pursuit and hard hitting. If we teach hitting and pursuit foremost, we must teach one sound defense thoroughly. Then we will add two companion defenses, similar in nature, and utilize the same techniques and containing unit. The differences in the companion defenses are purely in alignment. By utilizing our primary defense and two companion defenses, we can confuse the offensive blocking rules and still keep our defensive teaching relatively simple. This philosophy will always keynote simplicity, hitting and pursuit. By keeping this philosophy and technique constant, and without resorting to stunts, we can confuse the offensive team's blocking rules.

To explain this fully, let us look at the offensive right guard. We want to give him this look. First, having a defensive man play on his inside eye three feet off the line of scrimmage. Second, having the defensive man in the same position, but as close to the ball as possible coming across the line of scrimmage. Third, having the same defensive man on the outside shoulder, cracking through to the outside. Only three basic position—each time the offensive right guard approaches the line of scrimmage, he knows that the defensive man playing on him will be in one of three positions. If we can keep the offensive lineman from being unsure of where the defensive man is going to be, and what technique he is going to use, he will be more likely to make a mistake.

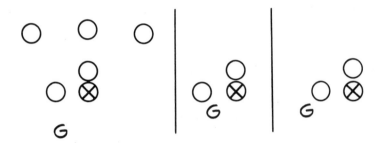

POUND THEM INTO SUBMISSION

Because of our excellent physical condition and our mental toughness, we expect to out-hit every team that we play. Our players are sold on this idea. They realize that some teams may out-finesse us, or have a smoother working machine, but none are going to out-hit us. We sell the theory that all teams will hit with us for the first quarter, but if we continue to pound and hit, our toughness and great pride will get to them. We want legal contact by our defensive players on every single play, if possible. We will never take the easy way. The more contact we have, the better we like it. We are mentally pre-pared for contact from the opening whistle until the final gun. We want our players sold on the idea that football is a tough contact sport. There is no greater way to play this game than with the sound of cracking helmets against pads. Our players are working, living and practicing all week long for the opportunity to play on Saturday and pound the opposition into submission.

DON'T MAKE MISTAKES

We feel that football is a game of mistakes. The team that generally makes fewer mistakes will win. Mistakes fall into many different classifications. A fumble recovered by your opponent on their 20-yard line is a mistake which may cost you a scoring opportunity or a touchdown. A pass in the flat, intercepted on the opponent's 20-yard line, may cost you two touchdowns; the touchdown that you may have scored, and the one run back 80 yards for a touchdown by your opponent.

We want each player so knowledgeable of our defensive philosophy, and so confident in our defensive ability that he believes the other team will make the mistake.

Because we are a defensive football team, our offense is geared to place our defensive unit in the proper field position. Therefore, our offensive team is very conservative. We will never take chances or gamble on any trick-play in our own territory. The objectives of our offensive team are: (1) score when the defensive team gains possession of the football on the opponent's side of the field, and (2) pick up a number of first downs so we will be in a favorable position to punt the ball deep into the opponent's territory and let our defensive team go to work. Our offensive team is designed to compliment our defensive team.

We want our defensive team to help the opposition to make mistakes. We believe this can be accomplished in the following ways:

1. Hit viciously on each play to encourage fumbles.
2. Second and third tackler on a gang tackle should reach and try to pry the ball loose from the ballcarrier.
3. Through scouting, be keenly aware of tendencies in unusual situations. An example of this may be third down, long yardage, screen pass attempt which we will try to pick off.

4. Keep the offensive team guessing where we will be on each play.

TALK ON THE DEFENSE

We want spirited enthusiasm at all times on our defensive unit. We want our defensive players talking to each other at all times. We like our linebackers to go to each defensive lineman, pat him on the back, and talk to him about the next play. We want our secondary unit talking all the time, before the ball is snapped, during the play and after the play. We want noise from all players on the defensive unit. Silence will not be tolerated. They should talk to the man on each side of them. If they have nothing to say, they should recite the Gettysburg Address. Congratulations should be given to the player who made the first contact. We urge our ballplayers to encourage each other constantly by chatter and a pat on the back for a job well done. After a game each player should not only be physically exhausted, but hoarse as well. A team without noise is a dead team. We have, at times, stopped a defensive scrimmage to practice talking! Talking by the defensive team should be encouraged and practiced until it becomes a habit. *Talking is important: you must practice it.*

CLAP ON THE DEFENSE

The best way to illustrate how we feel about this is to tell a little story. Two years ago we were undefeated going into our fifth game against a fifth-place team. We were a solid favorite. In the first quarter we were hit with two 50-yard pass plays off a double fake in the backfield for touchdowns. With two conversions, the score was now 14–0. No team had scored more than seven points against us that year until then, and the team was visibly shaken.

After their second touchdown, they kicked off to us again and we moved the ball back to the 30-yard line. The offense ground out two first downs and then was forced to punt. We barely got the punt off, and the opposition took over on their own 30-yard line. Our defensive unit went into the game, but you could see that the spark just wasn't there.

Our opponents made two first downs, and then we called a time out. We sent a substitute linebacker into the game, a little spark plug of a kid. As soon as he got into the game, he started clapping his hands in encouragement for the team as he waited for the opponents to line up on the ball. On the first play, he made a vicious tackle inside the end on an inside sweep. It was a beautiful hit; you could hear the thud of the pads. When we broke from our defensive huddle, he started clapping again. The other linebacker started clapping also. It was contagious. The ends, tackles, guards and secondaries also began clapping while they waited for the opponents to line up on the ball. We stopped the next play cold as well. Our entire bench now got up and started clapping on the sidelines. The clapping seemed to bring about a revived spirit.

We gained possession of the ball and moved in for a score just before the half, making the score 14–6 at the half. For the remainder of the game, our defense was tremendous. The opposition was held to eight yards' rushing for the remainder of the game, and we went on to win the game 18–14.

Since that ball game, our defense will clap from the time they break from their huddle until the opponent puts the ball into play. We firmly believe that clapping along with a lot of chatter helps to bring about the pride, spirit and unity required of championship football players.

ABSOLUTE DISCIPLINE

We believe that in order to have a great football team, you must have absolute discipline. This is the number one characteristic of any great football team. You can never have men hitting from week to week with the highest point of impact without it. We will not go into discipline in detail. In James Bonder's book, "How to Be a Successful Football Coach," * chapter 5 details the subject as thoroughly and as well as any material I have ever read.

Our feelings about discipline are these. Football coaching is one of the last dictatorships in our society, but it is a dictatorship with consent. No boy has to be on that football practice field; he may leave at any time. But if he chooses to be a member of the varsity football team, he must conform completely to the rules, standards, and policies that the coaching staff dictates. There are no exceptions.

SICK THEM ON THE SCORER

We have found that most high school football teams generally have one player who is the key to their offense. Normally, he is a backfield man, but on occasion, he may be an end. Through scouting, we will determine which player we must stop to win the football game. This is the man we will sick the team on, in practices the week preceding the game. We will not change any of our individual defenses to compensate for the ballcarrier's presence. Our team will be keenly aware of the whereabouts of this individual on each play. We will build this one player up, day by day, throughout the week preceding the game. We will exaggerate his size, speed, and ability. We want our team to know that this one man could walk on air!

This is done by the following:

1. During the week at defensive meetings, display the key man's name on the blackboard, with an enumeration of his accomplishments and abilities.
2. Emphasize to the team that if anyone has the ability

---

* James B. Bonder, *How to Be a Successful Coach* (Englewood Cliffs, N.J.: Prentice-Hall, Inc., 1959).

to stop our win streak or beat us single-handedly, it is this football player.

3. If there is a picture of him available, place it in the football room.
4. In black magic-marker, make signs bearing the boy's name. On Wednesday of the week of the game, place ten of these signs throughout the school. On Thursday, place 20 more, and on Friday 20 more. In this way, the team will be reminded of the man they have to stop.
5. When running the foreign team against the first string defense in practice, place one of the assistant coaches in this ballplayer's position. This helps to emphasize that player.
6. Build up almost a hatred for this player by Saturday.

On game day, we must feel that our men are ready to stop the opposition's scorer cold. Through our experience over the years, we will hold the back to very little yardage. In 1965, Northport was playing a key conference rival. Our opponents had a top back with good size, 6'2", 215, and he held the league sprint record for the 100-yard dash. He was a fine football player, and a tremendous threat to break open a game at any time.

The preceding week, we had prepared the team to meet this great back. We were mentally prepared to stop him cold. Unfortunately, during the week in practice, this back had received a minor injury, and he did not start the game. In the first quarter, we went ahead 6–0. With about two minutes to go in the half, the opposition had driven down to the two-yard line, with first and goal. Our defense seemed down, and it was apparent that they were going to score. They called time out, and the back we had keyed our team for all week came off the bench. There was a sudden rejuvenation in our defensive team as they saw the boy come into the game. They began jumping up and down clapping and shouting, "There he is!" For four downs he pounded the line and was met savagely by our defense. We eventually went on to win the game 6–0.

This illustration points out that mentally preparing our defensive unit to take on the opposition's chief scorer can stop him cold.

HOW TO COACH FOR THE BIG PLAY

Many high school football games are decided by just a couple of plays. We have seen films of games in which the elimination of perhaps three or four plays would make it virtually impossible to distinguish a winner. When singled out, these plays are generally the result of an outstanding performance by one player. We call such a crucial play, where an individual performance may change a ball game, the home run. We believe these individual plays, which may occur several times during a ball game and may change its outcome, are so important that we try to coach for them.

We try to sell our team the idea that the great football player will consistently come up with the home run, the big play. A close football game is decided by a number of crucial plays, plays which affect the outcome of the game. We tie the home run in with our defensive team. It is defined in this way: "A great performance on an individual play which is above and beyond the normal responsibilities on the football field." We list some of these unique plays as follows:

1. On a crucial third down play, nailing the passer before he has a chance to throw.
2. An extraordinary effort to be in a position to make a tackle on the field where the defensive player has no right to be.
3. Crashing through three men to make a tackle.
4. A great individual effort to stop the ballcarrier from making an important first down.
5. Blocking a punt.

6. Hitting a ballcarrier so viciously that it causes him to fumble.
7. Any kind of individual performance which stops a touchdown.
8. A pass interception in a clutch situation.
9. Stealing the football from the ballcarrier.
10. Stopping any crucial yardage situation.
11. Blocking a field goal or extra point.
12. Hitting a pass receiver after he catches the ball so hard that he drops the ball.

In order to have home runs, you must talk about them. The team must be aware that individually they are expected to produce the home run. We like to emphasize these big plays when we are reviewing films. Many times we attribute the victory to an individual home run, and emphasize this fact to the entire team. *To have the big play, you must coach for it.*

TEACH SIMPLICITY AND PERFECTION

Because the type of football that we coach is aggressive and hard hitting, we want our team's complete concentration on movement and hitting. At no time do we want them to worry about what they must do in a given situation. Consequently, our defensive patterns and our offensive plays are kept to an absolute minimum. We will not teach anything that we will not consistently use in a game. To illustrate this, we would not put in a reverse play to use once in four games, nor a screen pass up the middle not used frequently. We prefer to spend our practice time on a basic offense and defense. Therefore, everything that we do during practice sessions is planned for well in advance. It is for a specific reason, and will be used. We like everything to be so simple that there can never be a question by any ballplayer as to what is expected of him.

We use four basic defenses, with no offshoots. This is all we will use defensively. We teach 13 running plays, and five pass plays offensively; that is all we will teach. What we do, we want to do so well that a player never has any question as to what to do in any given situation, or against any defense. Through constant repetition, lectures, theory, review of films, we want to enable each player to go through his assignments, both offensive and defensive, automatically and instinctively. Our players are so emotionally keyed up for each ball game that having to think about each individual assignment would distract from their ability to hit.

Everything we teach is as simple as we can possibly make it, and it is perfected to the highest degree attainable. Simplicity and perfection, that is the secret.

4

HOW TO TEACH PURSUIT
FOR A WINNING DEFENSE

Defensive football requires three basic ingredients. They are:

1. Tackling—the ability to hit hard and clean;
2. Pursuit—the ability to be in a position to gang tackle;
3. Gang tackling—the ability to hit in mass.

These three ingredients are vital to a sound defensive football team. We teach them in the same order given above.

Once our team's ability to tackle and gang tackle is perfected, then our major emphasis is on pursuit. We firmly believe that once sound basic techniques of pursuit are taught, each defensive football player develops a great desire to be in the proper position. Therefore, we define pursuit as the individual desire of the defensive player to make the tackle.

We teach pursuit by three methods, as follows:

1. Teach theory of sound defensive pursuit on the blackboard and through films.
2. Teach pursuit on the practice field with exact drills and individual instruction.
3. Use motivational devices and film analysis.

THEORY OF PURSUIT (on the blackboard)

We have five general rules which we want all our defensive football players to memorize and understand completely. We will go over them at defensive meetings, and have question and answer sessions until they are understood completely by every ballplayer.

Five Rules of Pursuit

The rules are as follows:

1. Never go behind a player to get to the play (Diagram 1).
2. Never take the easy way.
3. Never chase the play on the opponent's side of the scrimmage line.
4. Never penetrate deeper than the heel of the offensive lineman on a play away from you.
5. Don't catch the play from behind; get in front of it.

We teach four different types of pursuit, and we teach them all through the use of diagrams. They are:

1. Up the middle pursuit (Diagram 1)
2. Off the tackle pursuit (Diagram 2)
3. End sweep pursuit (Diagram 3)
4. Pass completion pursuit

Pass completion pursuit is impossible to diagram, but we feel we can explain it in this way: As soon as the ball leaves the passer's hand, each defensive player must sprint to the area in which the ball will come down. We practice this every day, and emphasize that each player must start towards the ball no matter what distance, and be close to it when it comes down.

MIDDLE PURSUIT

Left End: Takes step across line of scrimmage, reads play, checks for reverse or counter, and then angles through the safety position, being the last man in the pursuit angle. Becomes leverage man.

Left Tackle: Delivers blow, reads play, and pursues the play up the middle, one yard behind the linebacker.

Left Linebacker: Takes one step up, reads the play, and

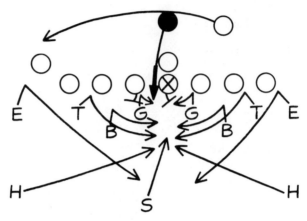

Diagram 1
Middle Pursuit

moves toward the middle directly behind his guard, being in a position to make the initial tackle.

Left Guard: Delivers the blow, reads the play, and reacts accordingly, attempting to jam the tackle individually.

Right Guard: Delivers blow, reads the play, fights to get to the ballcarrier and make the tackle.

Right Linebacker: Steps up, reads the play, pursues one yard play behind right guard, and is in a position to make the tackle.

Right Tackle: Delivers blow, reads the play and pursues one yard behind the linebacker.

Right End: Steps up, reads the play, checks for reverses or counters, and pursues through the safety position, being the last man in the pursuit angle.

Left Halfback: Reads his key, finds the ball, comes up quickly from the outside in, to be in a position to make the tackle.

Safety: Reads the center, finds the ball, commits quickly up the middle to make the tackle.

Right Halfback: Reads his key, finds the ball and pursues

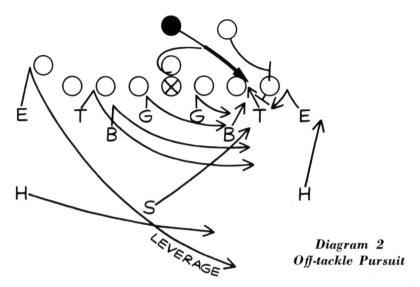

Diagram 2
Off-tackle Pursuit

quickly to the inside from the outside in to be in a position to make the tackle.

OFF-TACKLE PURSUIT

Left End: Steps across the line of scrimmage, reads the play, checks for reverses or counters, and pursues through the safety position, being the last man in the pursuit angle. He becomes leverage man and stays as deep as the ball in the backfield and crosses the line in his offside pursuit when the ball crosses the line.

Left Tackle: Delivers blow, reads the play, then pursues behind his line of scrimmage, being one yard behind the linebacker.

Left Linebacker: Reads his key, finds the ball and pursues rapidly to off-tackle hole.

Left Guard: Delivers blow, reads his key and pursues play one yard behind defensive right guard.

Right Guard: Reads key, delivers blow, and fights through to be in a position to make the tackle.

Right Linebacker: Reads key, fights to make tackle.

Right End: Reads key, finds play, and closes off-tackle hole viciously.

Left Halfback: Reads key, finds ball, pursues diagonally across the field being in a position to back up safety and defensive right halfback.

Safety: Reads key, finds ball and comes up quickly from the inside out being in position to make the tackle.

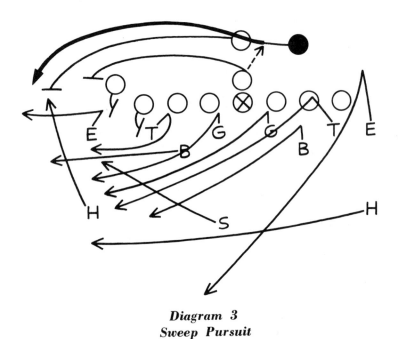

Diagram 3
Sweep Pursuit

Right Halfback: Reads key, finds ball, comes up hard from the outside in to be in position to make the tackle.

SWEEP PURSUIT

Left End: Steps up, reads key, and strings out play keeping the ballcarrier parallel with him.

Left Tackle: Delivers blow, reads key, spins out of the block by the end and pursues play at approximately a two-yard angle behind the line of scrimmage.

Left Linebacker: Reads play, fights quickly to the outside and comes up to meet the play.

Left Guard: Delivers blow, reads key, pursues to the outside two yards behind the line of scrimmage.

Right Guard: Delivers blow, reads key, pursues play to the outside one yard behind left guard.

Right Linebacker: Reads key, pursues play to opposite sideline at a four-yard depth.

Right Tackle: Delivers blow, reads key, pursues play on a 45 degree angle being in position to cut off the ballcarrier. He does not chase the play, but pursues on his side of the line of scrimmage.

Right End: Steps, reads key, checks for reverses or counters, and pursues through the safety position being in position to be the last man on the pursuit angle. Becomes the leverage man when ball crosses line of scrimmage.

Left Halfback: Reads key, comes up quickly forcing play from the outside in.

Safety: Reads key, finds ball, and comes up quickly from the inside out.

Right Halfback: Reads key, finds ball, moves laterally across the field being in position to back up the left halfback and safety.

MOTIVATIONAL DEVICES

We use two motivational devices which we believe to be a great asset in teaching pursuit. Our coaching staff has gone so far as to say that these two devices are really our game pursuit.

Tackling Chart

The first device is our tackling chart (Diagrams 4-5). The tackling chart is designed to be as simple as possible. We

NAME	THIS GAME			TOTALS TO DATE		
	Skull	Tackle	Part Tackle	Part Tackle	Tackle	Skull
Ahrenhold, Frank						
Bernath, Pete						
Beytin, Jeff						
Bologna, Frank						
Brenner, Bruce						
Campo, Mark						
Dillahunt, Mark						
Drago, Glenn						
Drago, Jim						
Farabaugh, Tom						
Fisch, Joe						
Fisher, Dave						
Frawley, Pat						
Grim, Will						
Grim, William						
Kelly, Don						
Koepper, Bob						
Kopke, Randy						
Luciano, Pete						
Madden, Bob						
Manley, Brian						
McCaffrey, Jerry						
McGuire, Bill						
Morgan, Kelly						
Niemczyk, Steve						
Nugent, Tom						
Parker, Wells						
Pelligino, Ray						
Pizzino, John						
Raimondo, Lou						
Rogers, Roy						
Sawka, Mike						
Tartamella, Len						
Wilson, Dave						
Zaleski, Larry						
Mickey, Ross						

NORTHPORT HIGH SCHOOL
VARSITY TACKLING CHART

Diagram 4
Tackling Chart

NAME		THIS GAME			TOTALS TO DATE		
NORTHPORT HIGH SCHOOL VARSITY TACKLING CHART — COMMACK		Skull	Tackle	Part Tackle	Tackle	Part Tackle	Skull
Ahrenhold, Frank			3	3	28	24	5
Bernath, Pete			1	3	5	5	
Beytin, Jeff	I.	*	1	1	9	6	3
Bologna, Frank	T. P.T.	**	5	6	31	25	6
Brenner, Bruce							
Campo, Mark							
Dillahunt, Mark							
Drago, Glenn							
Drago, Jim							
Farabaugh, Tom							
Fisch, Joe			4	3	27	20	6
Fisher, Dave	F.	*	2	1	24	19	10
Frawley, Pat							
Grim, Will	BLK. T. P.T.	***	4	3	14	10	4
Grim, William			3	3	5	7	
Kelly, Don							
Koepper, Bob				2		2	
Kopke, Randy							
Luciano, Pete	T.	*	5	4	24	27	4
Madden, Bob							
Manley, Brian				2		2	
McCaffrey, Jerry					3	5	
McGuire, Bill			1		1		
Morgan, Kelly				1		1	
Niemczyk, Steve	I.	*	1	2	21	19	9
Nugent, Tom			2	2	18	17	4
Parker, Wells							
Pelligino, Ray							
Pizzino, John			2	1	5	3	1
Raimondo, Lou			2	2	4	4	
Rogers, Roy	F. T.D.	**	3	3	22	24	8
Sawka, Mike							
Tartamella, Len							
Wilson, Dave	PASS 2	*	3	2	25	19	6
Zaleski, Larry				2		2	
Mickey, Ross			1	2	2	2	

Diagram 5
Tackling Chart After Fifth Game

are interested in only two things—tackles and part-tackles. The left side of the chart indicates the last game played, and the right side of the chart is an accumulation of all games to that date. The chart is placed throughout the school and displayed for the entire week, and then replaced by the new tackling chart the following Monday.

The tackling statistics are gathered in three ways:

1. Through game films.
2. On a chart kept by a manager on the field during a game.
3. By a duplicate chart kept by another official in the press box. All three sets of statistics are compiled to gain an accurate count and put on the tackling chart.

Full tackles are awarded for the first player to make contact with the ballcarrier. Part tackles are awarded to any ball player who gets onto the pile and gets a piece of the ballcarrier on each play. We are very generous in issuing part tackles, since we stress the fact, in pursuit and gang tackling, that each player will receive recognition for being part of the tackle.

We place great emphasis on our tackling chart. A player who does not consistently have a decent number of part tackles will be benched, and each player understands this. This in itself motivates each player to get in on every tackle, and certainly improves gang tackling and great pursuit.

Skull and Crossbones

We use an incentive system, as do many fine football teams. For us the symbol of defensive excellence is the skull and crossbones, and it is presented on Tuesday following a game. Helmets are collected on Tuesday and the coaching staff places the awarded skull decal on the helmets. This is a great motivational tool, with tremendous pride attached. The principle is similar to the placing of enemy insignia on the side of

Diagram 6
Skull and Crossbones

fighter plane aircraft. Players without a skull and crossbones will consistently strive to achieve this coveted award.

We cannot emphasize enough that the combination of a tackling chart and the skull and crossbones symbol has a tremendous influence upon our defensive team. High school students want and need this recognition and competition among themselves.

Skull and crossbones decals are awarded after each ball game for the following achievements:

1. Most tackles by any member of the defensive line or linebackers. If there is a tie, both players are awarded skulls.
2. Most part tackles by the defensive line or linebackers. Again, if a tie results, both players are awarded a skull.
3. Most tackles by a player in the secondary. A tie again results in two awards.
4. Most part tackles by a player in the secondary. A tie results in two awards.
5. Recovery of a fumble.

6. A pass interception.
7. Knocking the passer down twice in one game.
8. Scoring on the defense.
9. Blocking a punt.
10. Blocking an extra point or field goal.
11. A great individual defensive play as determined by the coaching staff.

The column on the near left is our award incentive system. This is a decal issued on Tuesday following the game, awarded for specific defensive play. We list the number of skulls a player has earned in the left column, and his accumulation of skulls in the right column. This chart, of course, leads to increased competition throughout the season. A large trophy is awarded at the annual football banquet to the defensive player accumulating the greatest number of skulls for the season.

The most important point in making any incentive system effective and successful is that it must have complete emphasis. Importance and status must be placed on it. It must be recognized by the fans, faculty, the student body, and the local newspapers. At every opportunity, the coach must play up the system to the newspapers.

We believe unquestionably that tackling charts and the skull incentive system will immediately help produce better gang tackling and pursuit.

DO NOT USE MORE THAN TWO CHARTS

We have seen coaches use many different types of charts; hit charts, area charts, pass reception charts, interception charts, kick-off coverage charts, honor rolls, fumble recovery charts. I personally had the experience in college of being confronted with many different charts after each ball game, and the importance of each diminished with the quantity! When a ball player comes in to look at the charts and there are six or seven of them, his determination is hampered, and he looks for the one chart in which he may have excelled to satisfy him. By having only one chart to check the ball player knows immediately just what we consider to be important in defensive football; namely tackling, gang tackling, and pursuit.

The tackling chart we use in conjunction with the incentive system of skull and crossbone awards gives us a fairly complete evaluation of our defensive unit.

YOU MUST HAVE FOUR DEFENSES, ONE BASIC

The first defense that a defensive football team must have should be their overall defense. It should be balanced and sound. It should have a three-deep secondary, because this makes for simple adjustments to split ends and flankerbacks. This defense should be used in all situations when the defensive signal caller is in doubt about what kind of play the offense will use. It should cover runs internally and outside. It should have good pass coverage. It is the defense called in most normal situations, and the defense that must be taught first.

The entire defensive philosophy including techniques and adjustments should be taught in this defense, and all of these basic techniques must be perfected. The team should feel that the entire defensive plan revolves around this defense, and that all other defenses just supplement it.

The second defense required should be a first down defense that plays tough from tackle to tackle, and is used to jam the offense either in stopping the play for no gain or limiting the gain to one or two yards. The reason we use this special defense for first down situations is that most high school teams will run a majority of first down plays inside or from tackle to tackle. This, of course, will also be determined through scouting.

This special defense should utilize the same techniques as

our basic defense, the main difference being that we are applying pressure from tackle to tackle in hopes of disrupting the normal three-yard average of the offense. We would like the offense to be a second down and eight, second and nine or second and ten yardage situation. This defense should also have a strong containing unit so as to never allow the long gain.

The third defense we use is a long yardage defense. This defense should be used in second and long yardage situations or in third down and six or above. It should cover passes, draws, screens and reverses, and should have a good pass rush.

The fourth defense required is a goal line defense. This defense should be used *only* inside the eight-yard line. It should never be used outside your own eight-yard line with the exception of a very crucial short yardage situation. This defense must be taught thoroughly and completely.

It is possible to have a fifth defense, a "Save-the-game" defense. We do not teach this defense, as we feel we can adjust our long yardage defense by moving the linebackers and secondaries back five yards, and thus we save a great deal of precious practice time.

The four defenses that we use will be covered thoroughly in the next four chapters.

5

A NEW APPROACH TO
THE WIDE TACKLE SIX

Our basic defense that we use is a wide tackle six. This defense is our overall defense and the defense that we teach first. All techniques involved are used in all other defenses in our system. Our line-up on the wide tackle six is pretty much identical with most wide tackle sixes. We feel that the big change we have made is in the individual techniques. We differ greatly in our theory of the defensive guards, defensive tackles and defensive ends. Our ends will never penetrate across the line of scrimmage unless the play shows pass. Our tackles will not hit the end, but will crash down with reckless abandon on the tackle, pitching him to the inside. Our defensive guards, also called floating guards, line up three to four feet off the line of scrimmage and move laterally, almost to the point of being linebackers. The individual assignments for this defense are as follows:

PLAY OF THE DEFENSIVE END

Defensive ends line up one yard outside of the offensive end; the outside foot back in an upright position. Read the flow of the near halfback. If the near halfback dives, close on the end, look to stop the off-tackle play. If the near halfback comes at you, move one step to the sideline laterally along the line of scrimmage. If the flow goes away, close to the inside watching for counters, reverses or ends around, then pursue the play. If sweep shows, do not penetrate. Move laterally, keeping the ballcarrier even with you, hand-fighting

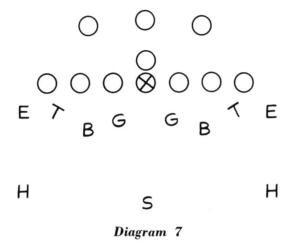

Diagram 7

the interference. It is a slow down maneuver. Do not come across and do not penetrate. The job is twofold:

1. Close the off-tackle hole if it shows off-tackle power. If the end blocks out, close from the outside in. If the play shows sweep, move laterally and slow the play down *staying on your feet* so pursuit and linebackers and outside halfback can make the tackle. The end must hand-fight, not commit to either side, outside or inside. The ball should be kept squarely in front (Diagram 8).

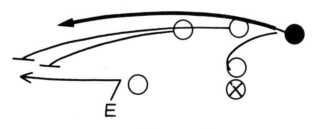

Diagram 8
End Playing Sweep

2. If play shows drop-back pass, drop off five yards into flat play pass defense. Pick up any receiver in your area. If none, look to the middle to help out. If play shows sprint-out or roll-out type of pass play, commit and force passer to throw the ball. Try to keep him to the inside. Do not let him run outside of you. When rushing the sprint-out pass play, rush to the outside of the block of the fullback and keep hands high, tackling from the head down. The end must also be aware, on drop-back passes, of reading the screen pass, and must come up accordingly and make the tackle. The play of defensive right end is identical to the left, only mirrored.

PLAY OF THE DEFENSIVE TACKLE

Defensive tackle will line up on the inside eye of the offensive end, as close to the line of scrimmage as possible without being offside. He should line up on a 45 degree angle facing the hip of the tackle. At the first movement of the tackle's hand, he should crack down through the tackle, aiming at the point where the quarterback lined up. He should stay low to the ground and explode through the tackle. The tackle's first responsibility is to stop the dive. If the tackle fires out at him, he should force the tackle back, delivering a blow, and continue penetrating through him. In many cases, the tackle will go out after the linebacker and giving the defensive tackle a free shot into the backfield, grab as many legs as he can, and find the ballcarrier. His path is always down and through the spot where the quarterback lined up. If the flow goes away, he must stop his charge and pursue the play on his side of the line of scrimmage. He is not to chase the play in back of the offensive team's line of scrimmage. *His angle of pursuit must be back behind his own defensive line,* forcing the play back towards the middle (Diagram 9).

If the play shows drop-back pass, the tackle must alter his charge and rush the passer. On all plays to his outside, the end

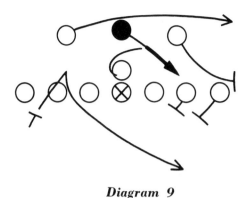

Diagram 9

will block down on him. As the tackle feels the block of the
end, he must stop his charge and drop his inside foot back,
making a complete spin, giving ground if necessary and
fighting to the outside. He must pick himself off the ground
and fight to the outside (Diagram 10). The end has an excellent block at this man, and he must give ground and make a
complete spin. He will not catch the play going around the
end's block. As he crashes down the line in his normal charge,
he should be aware of a trap block by the offside guard. As he
reads this, he should fight back to his inside, playing the trap-
per's inside shoulder back towards the middle of the line, giving

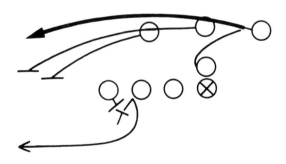

Diagram 10

Diagram 11

ground if necessary (Diagram 11). If the end and tackle double team him, he should fight through one of the two, depending on the flow of the play. If the flow is to the outside, he should fight through the end. If the flow is inside the tackle, he should fight to get to the inside of the tackle's helmet, giving ground if necessary but getting to the point of attack with the rest of the pursuit. The right tackle play is identical, only mirrored.

PLAY OF THE DEFENSIVE GUARD

Play of the defensive left guard: The left guard lines up three feet off the line of scrimmage on the inside eye of the offensive right guard. He is in a balanced three-point stance, keying the offensive fullback. He will split up to three feet with the offensive guard. If the offensive guard splits more than three feet, he will move out with him. As soon as the offensive guard takes a stance, he will jump back to the inside, right, outside shoulder of the center and penetrate through the gap. His normal stance is three feet off the ball, and keying through the fullback. As the ball is snapped, his charge is directed

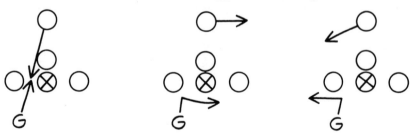

Diagram 12

at the offensive right guard delivering the blow. He will read the flow of the fullback. If the fullback comes directly at him, he will get as low as possible and penetrate through the gap at the fullback (Diagram 12). If the fullback's flow is to the right of the defensive guard, he will alter his charge, aiming directly at the center and expecting to meet the block of the center. With his right arm, he will deliver a blow at the center's helmet, fighting to keep the helmet to his inside, giving ground if necessary. He will pursue the play laterally behind the line of scrimmage. He must beat the block of the center, and keep the center's helmet to his inside. If the fullback movement is towards the defensive guard's left, he will expect the block of the guard, and will deliver the blow at the guard, fighting to

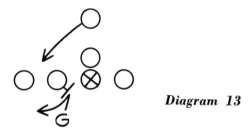

Diagram 13

keep the guard's helmet to his inside with his hands. He will then move laterally to his left, giving ground if necessary to get around the guard's block, pursuing the play laterally.

The defensive left guard must cover area from tackle to tackle (Diagram 13). Under no circumstances is he ever to be turned in either by the offensive right guard or the center. He must fight the block from either man. If the offensive right guard pulls, he is to fire at the gap and look to the inside for a trap block of the offside guard. If the play shows drop-back pass, he is to rush the passer through the gap between the center and the guard, being aware of a draw (Diagram 14). He must learn to read the blocks of the center, the right guard and the tackle, and react accordingly.

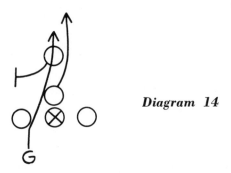

Diagram 14

The defensive left guard's responsibilities are as follows:

1. Stop the quarterback sneak.
2. Protect the gap between the center and the right guard.
3. Pursue the play to either side and fight to get to the ball-carrier.
4. Rush the passer.

Defensive right guard: The play of the defensive right guard is identical to that of the left guard.

PLAY OF THE LINEBACKER

Defensive left linebacker: The defensive left linebacker lines up three to four feet opposite the offensive right tackle. He lines up in a two-point stance and keys the far halfback (Diagram 15).

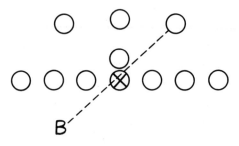

Diagram 15

He will cross-key and will be vulnerable to block the tackle coming straight at him. As the tackle comes at him, he will deliver a forearm blow, and react according to his key. If the far halfback flows toward the linebacker's side of the field, he will give ground laterally to the outside (Diagram 16). If this key dives, he will pursue to that side of the field. If the dive is coming to his side of the line, he will fight through the tackle blocking him, to make the tackle along with his defensive tackle. Of course, if the tackle fires out of him, his own defensive left tackle will get a free shot at the dive-man. If the offensive tackle blocks his tackle out, then the linebacker will have a free shot at the dive-man also. He should not be fooled by the fake to his side by the dive back, because he is reading his key which is the opposite halfback, and should be in position for any play going to his outside. The tackle has the initial responsibility of stopping the dive, not the linebacker.

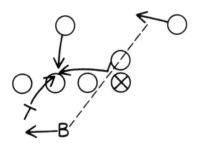

Diagram 16

If the play reads pass, the linebacker will drop back to the hook zone and play pass defense accordingly. As he drops back, he will watch for the draw and also read for the screen pass. The responsibilities of the linebacker are as follows:

1. Get a piece of the ballcarrier on every play from tackle to tackle.

2. Move laterally to his outside quickly, and be in a position to stop sweeps coming back to the inside.
3. Be a vital part of the pass defense.
4. Stop the draw and the screen.

The right linebacker is the same as the left, only mirrored.

PLAY OF THE DEFENSIVE SECONDARY

Defensive left halfback: We play our secondary up close. We want the defensive left halfback to be seven yards, two feet outside of his own left end. We want our secondary committing quickly on all running plays. The defensive left halfback has definite sweep responsibility to his side. We have experimented with the defensive left halfback keying the end, the tackle and the near side halfback. We found this most unsatisfactory for high school football players. We then experimented with the halfback keying the end and tackle. We found this a little too complicated. Eventually, we came up with the simple task of keying his side. We now have the left halfback keying only the end. He will also key the wingback if there is a wingback to his side. The defensive halfback lines up with his outside foot back and all his weight on his back foot. As he reads the key of the end, he will react accordingly. If the end blocks in, he will fire up quickly to the outside, and be in a position to make the tackle on the sweep. We have found that our defensive halfbacks, when drilled on this maneuver, become quite proficient at it. In many instances, they have made tackles two and three yards behind the line of scrimmage, passing the defensive end who is slowing the play down. He must always have outside leverage, and come up from the outside in, forcing everything inside of him. He must make tackles. He must never let anything go outside of him. If the end blocks out, he will fire up slightly to the inside, looking for the off-tackle play. He will always tackle from the outside in.

If the end releases downfield into the secondary, the half-back must play the play as a pass, and stay behind him. If the flow goes away in the backfield, he will play the end for a pass, and take a deep angle of pursuit across the field in the direction of the flow. If the play shows drop-back pass, he will retreat to his third of the field in a zone pass defense, never letting anyone get deeper than he does. We emphasize coming up and stopping the run quickly. Our defensive halfbacks take great pride in making tackles on the line of scrimmage, and also having many part tackles by being a part of the gang tackle. We realize it is possible with this philosophy to be beaten by a home run occasionally. But we feel that if he reads his key adequately, and learns to react instinctively, this will happen perhaps only once in a season.

If the end is split to his side of the field more than six yards, then he will have to play him man to man and will notify the safety accordingly. If a flanker-back is sent out to his side of the field, he will move out with the flanker and play him man to man if he is out further than six yards. He will adjust his key to the flanker-back notifying his safety, and the saftey will adjust his key to the strong side end.

Responsibilities of Halfback

The responsibilities of the defensive left halfback are as follows:

1. Read the key of the end.
2. Come up quickly on sweeps and make the tackle.
3. Come up quickly to inside, and become a part of the gang tackle.
4. React to pass plays in typical zone defense.
5. Pursue all plays to the opposite side of the field, and be in a position to cut off the ballcarrier.
6. Hit and enjoy hitting!

The play of the defensive right halfback is the same as the left, only mirrored.

Responsibilities of the Middle Safety

The middle safety is normally our best football player. He should be tall, quick, and have the ability to hit on the move. He lines up seven yards deep, head up with the center against a balanced set. He reads the block of the center. Whichever way the center blocks, he fires up quickly to the opposite side at an angle at the off-tackle hole, reading the play accordingly. As he is moving up, he will be looking at the end and the wingback (if there is one) for a possible pass move. Normally, the flow will come that way and he should be in a position to meet the off-tackle power play at the line of scrimmage. He will also be the forcing unit from the inside on sweeps. We want our safety tackling almost on the line of scrimmage from end to end. Therefore, on a sweep to the safety's left, the left halfback will fire up to the outside, turning everything in, and the safety will be firing up to the off-tackle hole, keeping the sweep between the halfback and the safety. The defensive right halfback will be coming on a deep angle of pursuit to cut off any possible breakthrough, and to catch any delayed receiver.

THE WIDE TACKLE SIX TOUGH DEFENSE

This defense is identical to the wide tackle six with but two exceptions:

1. The defensive guards line up tight, as close to the ball as possible, and penetrate through the inside gap of the guards.
2. Linebackers will play two feet off the ball now, and deliver a blow straight at the tackle.

The remainder of the defensive unit plays as it normally would in our regular wide tackle six. This defense is primarily used on short-yardage situations, and when the offensive team is making yards through the middle of the line.

6

COACHING THE SPLIT SIX— THE CHANGE UP

The split six is a pressure-type defense that we use in conjunction with our wide tackle six. We use it as a change of pace and on many first down plays. We feel that it gives us a great advantage in that most teams recognize us as a wide tackle six defensive team. In our wide tackle six or basic defense, we do a good deal of lateral moving, staying behind our own line of scrimmage. Many people have characterized us as a floating defense, and by use of the split six, we can come across the line of scrimmage with our guards and tackles putting pressure on the offense. We like to jump into this defense just as the offensive linemen take their stance. Our guards and linebackers change position just as this occurs (Diagrams 17 and 18). You can see by the diagrams that with the exception of the guards and linebackers (Diagram 19), both the alignments are almost identical. It shows very little difference to the offense, yet we have an entirely different concept of defense. We are not moving laterally, we are penetrating (Diagrams 20-21).

If we look at the initial alignment of the defensive tackle in both defenses, we find that they are almost identical. By looking at the charge of the defensive tackle of both the wide tackle six and the split six, we can see that while initially it seems the same, we get a completely different penetration (Diagram 22).

Although the offensive end has an easy block on the tackle of our wide tackle six, the block becomes very difficult when

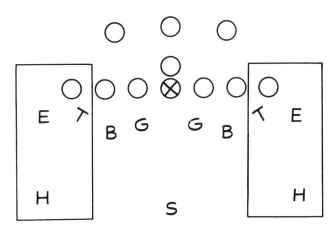

WIDE TACKLE

Diagram 17
Wide Tackle

Diagram 18
Split Six

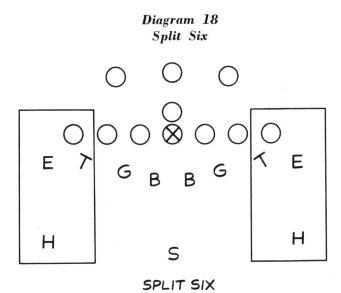

SPLIT SIX

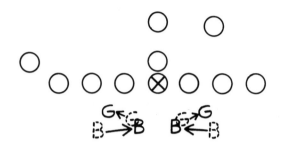

Diagram 19

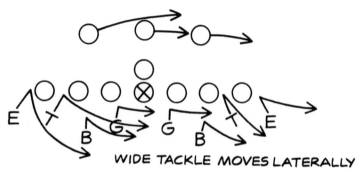

WIDE TACKLE MOVES LATERALLY

Diagram 20
Wide Tackle Moves Laterally

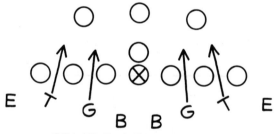

SPLIT SIX PENETRATES

Diagram 21
Split Six Penetrates

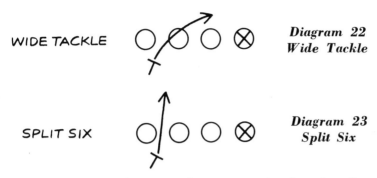

WIDE TACKLE

Diagram 22
Wide Tackle

SPLIT SIX

Diagram 23
Split Six

he penetrates straight across (Diagram 23). Also, the offensive tackle who has become accustomed to the defensive tackle crashing down and through his position, now has a tackle coming straight across in a different look. The offensive tackle now has a gap set look (Diagram 24), and must block down on the guard and play to his side of the line. If he does not, this will give the defensive guard a free shot into the backfield. This will occur frequently in an inferior high school football team. Also the probability of a fumble rises sharply as the defensive guard has a free shot.

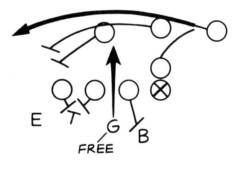

Diagram 24

We have found that this defense, when used infrequently and purely as a change, will cause confusion and blocking mistakes in the best of high school teams. We also find that the offensive guard has a problem in becoming used to the defensive guard playing off the line of scrimmage in our wide tackle six, and playing a control, floating, pursuing type of defense. When we change into this defense, and blow him through the outside gap, the guard is not prepared for this maneuver.

Now, if we look at this defense against a sweep, we can see that if one man is uncertain and does not block the correct man, or does not block it as a gap defense, we will have either a guard or tackle getting a free shot into the backfield or a freed-up linebacker (Diagrams 25-26).

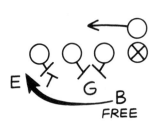

Diagram 25

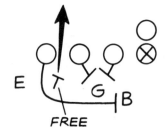

Diagram 26

We have also found that this defense is a good change-up defense against a sprint-out passer (Diagram 27). The onside end, or the end towards whom the quarterback is sprinting out, will come across and stop the play, or force the passer back inside. The defensive tackle and the defensive guard have excellent angles to beat their men and put pressure on the quarterback. When we use this as a pass defense, the offside end will drop back over the middle and pick up one third of the linebacker pass coverage (Diagram 28).

The individual defense assignments for the split six, as we call it, are as follows:

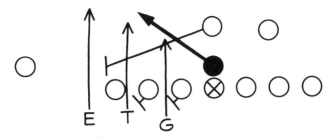

Diagram 27

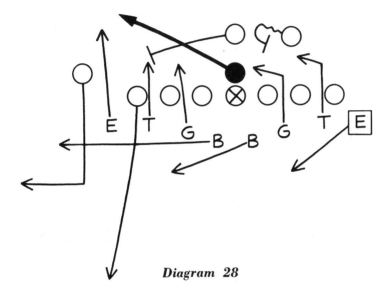

Diagram 28

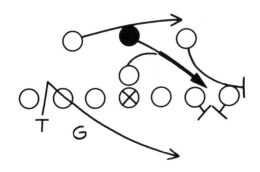

Diagram 29

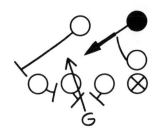

Diagram 30

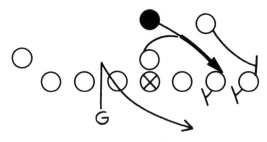

Diagram 31

PLAY OF ENDS

Left end: The left end plays identically as he does in our wide tackle six defense. This is detailed in Chapter 5.

PLAY OF TACKLES

Left defensive tackle: The left defensive tackle will line up between the tackle and the end, favoring the end slightly. His angle will be almost straight into the backfield as opposed to our wide tackle six where he is angled toward the tackle. At the first movement of the hand of the offensive tackle or end, the defensive tackle will penetrate straight across, shooting the gap. As soon as he crosses the line of scrimmage he will read the play. He should be aware of a possible trap block, and if he reads one, he should fight back to the line of scrimmage. If the right end blocks down on him, he will fight through the right end directing his charge out wide. If the tackle blocks out on him, he will direct his charge through the tackle and angle inside. If the end and tackle both block him, or double-team him, he will fight the end's block, disregarding the block of the tackle. As soon as he makes penetration, he should look for the play. If the play is coming to his side, he should fight through and put pressure on the ballcarrier and the blockers involved. If the play shows a run up the middle, he should stop his charge and fight back behind his own line of scrimmage, fighting to get to the ballcarrier and reacting up the middle. If the flow goes away from him, he should stop his charge and retreat behind the line of scrimmage, pursuing the play on his side of the line (Diagram 29). He should never chase the play in the opponent's backfield. If the play shows pass, he should rush the passer as hard as possible.

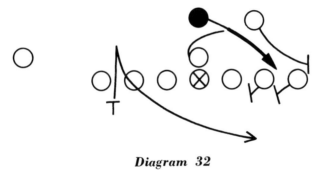

Diagram 32

Right defensive tackle: The play of the right defensive tackle is identical to that of the left defensive tackle, only mirrored.

PLAY OF GUARDS

Left defensive guard: The left defensive guard will split the gap between the offensive guard and the offensive tackle. He will line up as close to the ball as possible. He will favor the guard's shoulder just slightly. At the first movement of the offensive guard or tackle's hand, the defensive guard will penetrate through the gap. If the offensive guard blocks out at him, he will alter his charge in and through the guard, trying to read the play and determine where the ball will cross the line of scrimmage and then adjusting his charge accordingly. If the tackle blocks down on him (Diagram 30), he will alter his charge at and through the offensive tackle, trying to penetrate for depth and movement of the play. If the play goes to the other side of the line of scrimmage, he will stop his charge and retreat behind his own line of scrimmage, taking the proper angle of pursuit (Diagram 31). If neither the guard nor the tackle blocks him, he will pursue the play in the backfield of the offensive team, and he will get depth as quickly as possible, trying to locate the ball and break up the play. If the play shows pass, he will rush the passer aggressively (Diagram 33). He also should be aware of a trap block coming from the offside of the line. If both the guard and tackle block on him, he should disregard the guard's block and fight through the tackle's block (Diagram 34), penetrating on a wide angle.

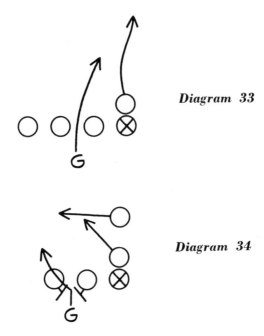

Diagram 33

Diagram 34

Defensive right guard: The play of the defensive right guard is the same as the left guard, only mirrored.

PLAY OF LINEBACKERS

Left linebacker: The left linebacker lines up three and a half feet off the line of scrimmage on the inside eye of the offensive guard. If the guard splits out more than two and a half feet, he will take his position in the gap. He will read through the center and quarterback to the far halfback. Both our linebackers still cross key in this defense, the same as they do in the wide tackle six (Diagram 35).

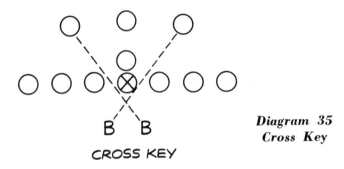

CROSS KEY

Diagram 35
Cross Key

The linebacker will not deliver a blow at the guard unless the play is coming right over him. In this case, he will fight to get below the block of the right guard or center and jam the play accordingly. His movement is determined completely by the path of the far halfback. If the halfback swings wide to his side, he immediately moves laterally to the outside. He does not waste time delivering a blow, but moves as quickly as possible to be in position to meet the halfback wherever he comes across the line of scrimmage. If the far halfback goes away from him, he will come right over the center, protecting the two middle holes, reading the play and reacting to it (Diagram 36). If the far halfback comes right over the center, then he will jam the play (Diagram 37).

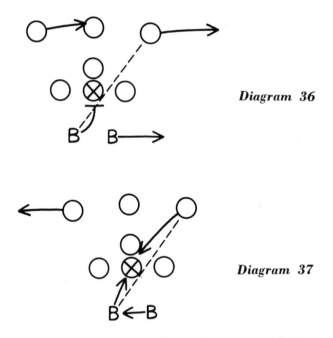

Diagram 36

Diagram 37

The linebacker must always be aware of the quarterback sneak, or fullback up the middle, and must be prepared to stop these plays. If the play shows pass, he will retreat back to the left hook zone (Diagram 38). As he retreats, he must be especially aware of the possible draw play, as this defense is vulnerable to it. He must also be aware of the possible screen pass.

Linebacker's Responsibilities

The linebacker's responsibilities are as follows:

1. Read the flow of the far halfback. If the play moves to his side of the line, move laterally to the off-tackle hole and then to the outside.
2. If the play comes up the middle, jam the play.
3. If the flow goes away, move over the center, protect the middle, and then pursue the play.

4. On the drop-back pass plays, move back to the hook zone, and play pass defense, being aware of a possible draw or screen.
5. On the sprint-out pass to his side, move laterally towards the flat and be in position to play pass defense.
6. On the sprint-out pass away from the linebacker, move to the middle zone. You have middle hook coverage.

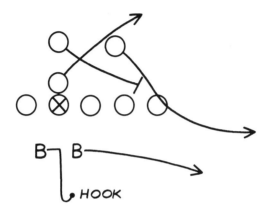

Diagram 38

PLAY OF THE SECONDARY

The play of the secondary is identical to our defensive secondary in the wide tackle six, with the exception that the defensive halfbacks must realize that our linebackers are now moved a man and a half to the inside, or closer to the center. This, therefore, tends to slow down reaction and pursuit to the outside. Consequently, on the split-six defense we teach our defensive halfbacks that they still must come up on end runs, and read their keys the same way; but they must realize that the linebacker's pursuit will be at least a step or two slower, and therefore they must be somewhat more conservative in coming up to the sweep to avoid missing a tackle or over-committing.

ADJUSTMENTS IN THE WIDE TACKLE
SIX AND THE SPLIT SIX

Keeping in mind simplicity and perfection, we try to keep adjustments to a minimum. We would rather be slightly out-manned than have one defensive player unsure of his exact responsibilities. The few adjustments that we do make are explained most carefully and practiced often. We have a three-deep secondary at all times, necessitating little adjustments on deep-pass coverage. The adjustments for both defenses are just about identical and are enumerated as follows:

On a split end to either side, the defensive end would drop off and play three by three (Diagram 39). On both these de-fenses the defensive tackle would now be playing outside of the tackle, and would have no immediate threat of a block to his outside. The end who has now dropped off would maintain his same responsibilities, and add to them the glance-in pass. He must also be aware of a comeback block by the split end. The defensive halfback would move out with the split end, and play him man to man if he was out more than six yards.

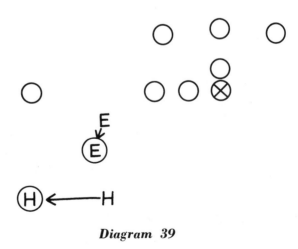

Diagram 39

On a floater to one side of the field, the halfback would again move over to be in position to cover him; the safety would move over one and a half full men to be in position to keep the tight end between himself and the halfback on his side (Diagram 40); the end would play his normal position but keep aware of the floater to his side and a comeback block.

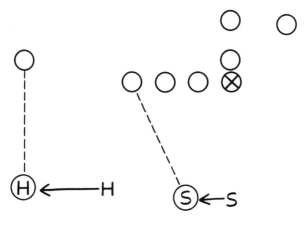

Diagram 40

The adjustment of the flanker to one side would be made completely by the secondary. This would give the offense a full power set to either side of the side of the flanker. The defensive team is taught to recognize a power set, to call it out, and expect the play to the strong side off-tackle hole or sweep. We make no adjustment from end to end unless, through scouting, we learn of a definite tendency when in this formation for the offensive team to run certain plays. In this case we may bring the offside linebacker over the middle, and move the strong side linebacker directly behind his tackle (Diagram 41).

On a three deep backfield or full house backfield, with any back going in motion, the adjustment we make will be purely in the secondary. The halfback to that side would pick up the man in motion, and the safety would move to that side to ad-

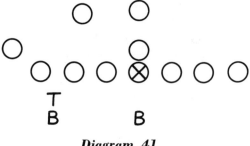

Diagram 41

just and be in position to pick up the tight end. The defense from end to end would make no adjustments, play normally with the exception of being conscious of the motion man, and would be in position to watch for a comeback block.

Adjustment by Guards if Split Out

This is covered on page 72.

If guard splits more than three feet, defensive guard will close and fire gap (Diagrams 42-43).

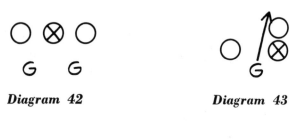

Diagram 42   *Diagram 43*

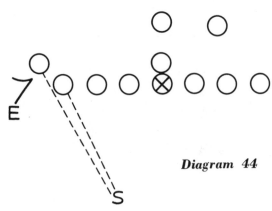

Diagram 44

Adjustment Against Close Wingback Outside End

End will line up outside wingback up to three yards and play the wingback as he would normally play the end (page 68). The safety will line up outside the wingback side guard and switch his key to the end and wingback, ready to react quickly to the off-tackle hole (Diagram 44).

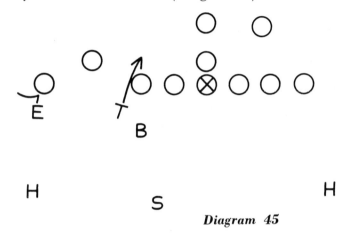

Diagram 45

Adjustment to the Tight Slot

If the tight slot end is split three yards or under the defensive end will play slightly outside of him and play normally (page 68). The defensive tackle will line up outside his tackle and fire at a position where the right halfback's position would have been. The safety will line up outside the slot side guard and adjust his key to the slot back. The left halfback will line up slightly outside the slot end and play normally (Diagram 45).

Adjustment to the Wide Slot

Against a wide slot the defensive end will drop off, play nose up, and play the slot as he would normally play the tight end. The defensive left tackle will take a deep charge at the normal right halfback position. The safety will play behind

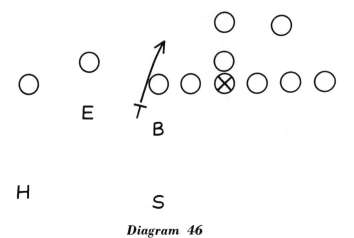

Diagram 46

his left linebacker and change his key to the slot. The halfback and safety will keep the end and the slot between them on a pass (Diagram 46).

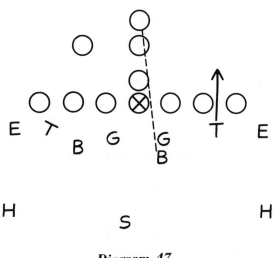

Diagram 47

Adjustment to the Power I

The only adjustments we make to a Power I are these: the right linebacker moves over behind his right guard and keys the tailback (deep back). The right tackle now cracks straight over the outside shoulder of the tackle. The safety moves over half a man towards strength of formation (Diagram 47).

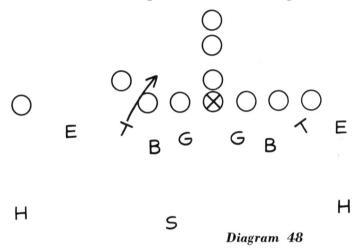

Diagram 48

Adjustment to I Wing Slot Right

End drops off to split end (page 68). Tackle crashes deeper than normal. Safety lines up outside guard and keys wingback. Right linebacker changes key to tailback. If the tailback goes away, he looks for wingback coming back (Diagram 48).

Motion from full house backfield is done by secondary only (Diagram 49).

Motion adjustment when there is a flanker, floater or wingback to either side, and only two deep running backs behind the quarterback, is as follows: When motion goes to either side by one of the remaining deep backs, the linebacker to the side of the motion would move laterally with the motion man, giving ground to approximately four yards. The offside line-

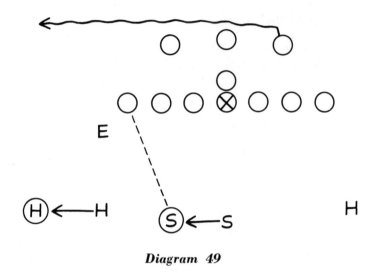

Diagram 49

backer would then move to a position of head-up on the
remaining back wherever he may be, and would key him (Diagrams 49-50). This adjustment would hold true in any situation
where there are two deep backs, one of whom is in motion,
giving us four defenders against four quick releasing receivers.

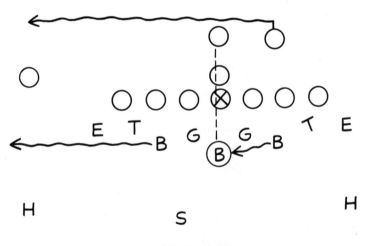

Diagram 50

These are the only adjustments that we teach, and we teach them thoroughly. Our philosophy dictates that we will never cheat unless the offensive team forces us to by completely over-shifting on our defense.

7

COACHING THE PRESSURE SIX
OR LONG-YARDAGE DEFENSE

The pressure six is the defense that we use in all situations where we expect a pass, or long-yardage plays such as an end sweep, draw, screen pass or reverse. In keeping with our philosophy of simplicity and easy adjustment, the alignment for this defense is a six-man line, as in our other two defenses. It requires very little change in technique, and looks similar in that the alignment is six men across, two linebackers, and a three-man secondary (Diagram 51).

In keeping with our premise that we try to teach players to beat their man, rather than fool them, we play an "in between" defense in long-yardage situations. The experts say

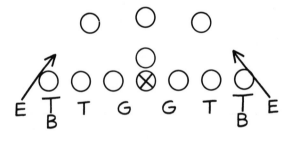

Diagram 51
Pressure Six

PRESSURE SIX

that the best way to play long-yardage situations or passing downs, is by rushing seven men and leaving four to defend in the secondary, or by rushing four men and leaving seven to defend in the secondary. They also point out that against a good passer, it is usually best to rush more men with immediate pressure, whereas against a poor passer it is best to rush few men and place more men in the secondary.

We disagree with this for high school football. We believe in balance at all times. We never want to get stung with a big play, and yet we realize we must put an adequate rush upon the passer. Therefore, we have developed a middle-of-the-road type of defense which has proven most satisfactory for us. This pressure defense puts good pressure on the quarterback by rushing six men. We feel that in high school you must place pressure on the quarterback. Most high school quarterbacks are not poised enough to throw continually well against pressure. We also feel that usually a high school quarterback, if given enough time to throw and complete security in his pocket, will be capable of picking out a receiver in a group of defensive secondary men.

SIX OBJECTIVES OF THE
LONG-YARDAGE DEFENSE

Our first objective in this defense, therefore, is to put adequate pressure on the quarterback. We will rush six men from good strategic points.

Secondly, we want to defend against end runs in long-yardage situations. An end run, in high school football, can many times break away for a long gain. This defense is very strong to the flanks.

Our third objective is to defend against the long pass. We keep three men deep in the secondary.

Our fourth requirement is to defend against special plays

such as the draw or the screen pass. We must concern ourselves with the screen pass, because if it is not adequately covered, it may result in a long gain. However, most high school teams will use the screen pass probably no more than twice in one game, and those that do, would be scouted, and defended against beforehand.

The fifth requirement for long-yardage defense is that we are capable of playing passes into the flat. We feel that most quarterbacks are inaccurate when throwing to delayed backs or throwing flair passes out of the backfield. This is a skill that requires poise, dedication and much practice time, and our feeling is that even the best high school quarterbacks are weak in throwing this type of pass. Admittedly, our two losses in the past three years have come from a tax on our flank through short passes. But a total of two out of 24 is not difficult to live with. We are going to have to see a great deal more bombardment in our flats before we change our thinking on it at this point.

Our sixth objective for long-yardage defense is to protect against the short pass over the middle. This is a difficult type of pass to complete because there are many things that can go wrong with this type of play; i.e., a quick receiver being held up on the line of scrimmage, a lineman getting in the path of a quarterback, or any type of bad throw resulting in an interception, this being the most vulnerable area for interceptions. Quarterbacks tend to keep away from the short or quick pass on long-yardage situations.

These objectives are listed in order of importance, we believe. Our pressure six defense is designed to work on each objective, giving one priority over six, and so on. Consequently, we want an excellent pass rush, and little coverage in the short middle.

Individual assignments and responsibilities are listed as follows:

PLAY OF THE END

Defensive ends: The defensive ends in our two basic defenses are normally in an upright two-point stance. We would like them to maintain this stance as long as they are proficient in getting a quick start towards rushing the passer. If they are unable to do this, we will place them in a three-point stance. They will line up two feet outside the offensive end. We want them close enough to the offensive end to try to dissuade him from going around our linebacker. He should make no contact with the offensive end, however. In our pressure six defense, the primary responsibility of the defensive ends is as a pass rusher. We want them to crack into the backfield as quickly as possible. We want them to knife in and get to the passer. We tell them that they have no outside responsibility, unless the play shows end runs. If this happens, they should flatten out their charge and try to contain it. First contact in the backfield is usually made by the near halfback, unless the halfback is a part of the pass pattern, and in this case the end will be met by the fullback.

The first time we call this defense, we want our defensive ends to crack right through the halfback, belting him as hard as possible, and then fighting to get to the passer. After the initial contact whenever we call this defense, we want the ends to do one of three things:

1. Rush right through them.
2. Fake inside and go outside (Diagram 52).
3. Fake outside and go inside.

By mixing up these three types of charges, we have had success in getting our ends to the passer. His three normal paths are drawn in the diagram below.

Responsibilities of the End

The responsibilities of the defensive end are:

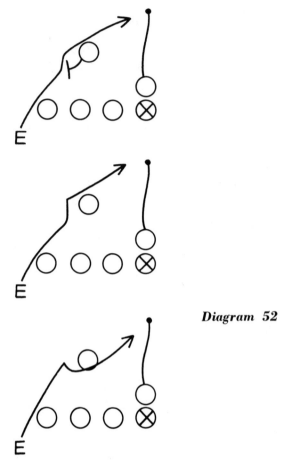

Diagram 52

1. Rush the passer as viciously as possible in a drop-back pass.
2. Keep the passer inside him if possible.
3. If the play shows end run, string out the play.
4. If the play shows off-tackle, close hard.
5. If the play shows roll-out or sprint-out to the end side, he must contain quarterback and cut off as much ground as possible. He must never get cut down.
6. If the play goes away, pursue play hard in the backfield.

PLAY OF THE TACKLE

Defensive tackle: The defensive tackle lines up as close to the line of scrimmage as possible. His initial point is the inside eye of the offensive tackle. On the first movement of the offensive tackle's hand, we want our defensive tackle to crack hard through the inside shoulder of the tackle, delivering a blow as he does so. We want him to rush the passer as hard as he can. As a change up on every third or fourth time we call this defense, we want our defensive tackles to fake inside and go over the outside shoulder. The defensive tackle's charge is illustrated below (Diagram 53).

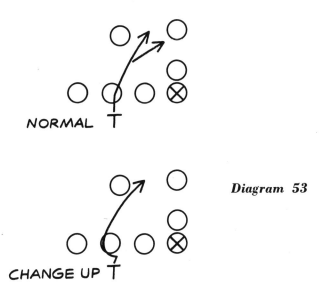

NORMAL

CHANGE UP

Diagram 53

Responsibilities of the Tackle

The responsibilities of the defensive tackle are as follows:

1. Rush the passer as hard as possible.
2. Be cognizant of a screen pass, and if he reads it, go with the flow of the play and try to stop it.

3. Be prepared to meet a draw play.
4. As soon as he penetrates into the backfield, determine whether it is a pass play. If not, pursue the play accordingly.
5. Get hands up high as soon as penetration is made into the backfield. Force the passer to throw over his hands.

PLAY OF THE GUARD

Defensive guards: The defensive guard lines up as close to the line of scrimmage as possible, on the inside shoulder of the offensive guard. At the first movement of the center or the guard, he will crack hard through the gap, delivering a blow at the offensive guard. He will make penetration as quickly as possible and rush the passer. His major responsibility is getting to the passer. He must also be prepared to check a draw play if it shows. As soon as he penetrates across the line of scrimmage, he should get his hands up high to put pressure on the passer. If a play develops away from him, he should stop his charge and take his proper angle of pursuit.

Responsibilities of the Guard

The responsibilities of the defensive guard are as follows:

1. Rush the passer quickly.
2. Be prepared to meet the draw play.
3. As soon as penetration is accomplished, throw hands up high and force the passer to throw over him.

PLAY OF THE LINEBACKER

On the pressure six defense, the linebacker will line up on the inside eye of the offensive end, four feet off the line of scrimmage. We want our linebacker to be close enough to the end to be able to deliver a blow at him, slow him down and still read the flow of the near halfback. He should key the near halfback, and on his first movement he will deliver a blow at the end. If the play shows drop-back pass, he should begin retreating to the hook zone, still keying the near side halfback. As he is retreating to the hook zone, he is carefully watching his flat. He has complete responsibility of any type of pass into the flat on his side of the field. He also has end run responsibility, and if the play shows sweep, he must move to the outside and string out the play. If any receiver moves into the flat, he must release from the hook zone and immediately go to cover the flat area. If the play shows sprint-out or roll-out pass to his side, he must go to the flat area and disregard the hook zone. If sprint-out or roll-out goes away from him, he must retreat and cover the middle hook zone area (Diagram 54). His normal movement is illustrated in this diagram below.

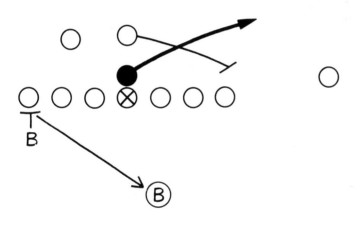

Diagram 54

Responsibilities of the Linebacker

Responsibilities of the linebacker are as follows:

1. Deliver a blow to the offensive end to slow him down.
2. Read the flow of the nearside halfback.

3. Retreat to the hook zone and be prepared to pick up any receiver in the flat.
4. Be responsible for all end runs to his side.
5. Be responsible for any screen pass to his side of the field.
6. Be prepared to help out on a draw play.
7. Cover any receiver in the flat on sprint-out or roll-out pass to his side.
8. On the sprint-out or roll-out, pass away from him. Cover the middle of the field hook zone area.
9. Read the play and pursue accordingly.

PLAY OF THE DEFENSIVE SECONDARY

The defensive secondary will play identically with the secondary of the wide tackle six defense. The only difference is that this is a long-yardage defense and we like our secondary to loosen up at least one and a half yards, and be cognizant of the long-yardage situation. But their initial keys and reactions remain the same.

8

COACHING GAP EIGHT
OR GOAL LINE DEFENSE

The gap eight is our goal line defense. We use this defense because:

1. It is easy to teach.
2. Responsibilities are cut and dried.
3. This defense cuts off the quarterback sneak and fullback up the middle, the two most common scoring plays on the goal line.
4. We can keep our secondary intact.
5. Our guards, tackles and ends remain in their same position.
6. We believe we can get the most penetration from this type of alignment.
7. We can blend our wide tackle six defense directly into the gap eight with no confusion (Diagrams 55-56).

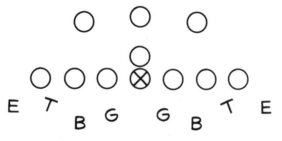

Diagram 55
Wide Tackle Six

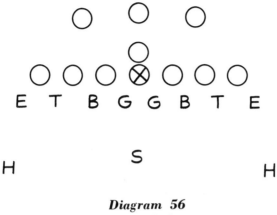

Diagram 56
Gap Eight

In our goal line defense, we are not teaching finesse; we are teaching savage contact. Our defensive team is taught that when we are in this defense, we are playing for keeps. There is no more room to recover. We must do it now! We explain to our team that if there is any weakness in our defensive team, it will show up in our goal line defense. We like to teach pride in not allowing the offense to make an inch over each individual's position. We drill our defensive team in the thought that *teams that make goal line stands, win championships!*

We like to take our own defensive unit and put them on their own three-yard line, and give the ball to the foreign team with four downs to score. We usually do this once each week for about five minutes of live contact. We tell the defensive unit we hope the offense scores so we can eliminate the weak link in the defense. The offense rarely scores, and we find this to be a good morale builder for the defense.

In order to have good goal line defense, we must have complete understanding of goal line theory by the defensive unit. We try to teach the following principles in the classroom before we teach actual techniques on the practice field.

ELEVEN PRINCIPLES OF GOAL LINE DEFENSE

1. When we are in a goal line defense, we are playing completely for penetration, not pursuit. Pursuit will do us no good.
2. We are defending a much shorter area, therefore our secondary can play in front of receivers.
3. We must substitute aggressiveness for finesse.
4. We cannot cover all possible receivers on the goal line. We must compensate for this by a tremendous rush by our eight defensive linemen. If the quarterback has time, we are in trouble.
5. Everyone must pinch hard to close up the gap inside them.
6. The weakest part of a goal line defense is a play run inside our defensive end. We must make our weakness our strength.
7. It is imperative that we get a home run (Big Play) down on the goal line.
8. Teams who make goal line stands win championships. Teams who do not, become also-rans.
9. Defensive halfbacks have outside responsibility; defensive ends do not.
10. The defensive line is responsible for stopping any back by a low charge. The safety is responsible for meeting a back who jumps over the line by hitting him squarely in the upper part of the chest with his helmet.
11. The safety is responsible for filling the off-tackle hole to either side (Diagrams 57-58).

FOUR-POINT STANCE—A MUST

On our goal line defense, we want all eight defensive linemen in a four-point stance rather than our normal three-point stance. This includes the defensive ends. We do this because we want our defensive linemen as low to the ground as pos-

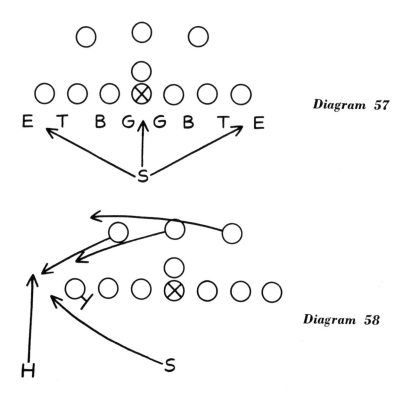

Diagram 57

Diagram 58

sible. We feel that there is a psychological advantage in being at least a foot lower than the offensive linemen. We want our players to be in a stance similar to a sprinter's stance, with the head a bit lower. The legs should be coiled under the body as if they were a spring ready to explode. We illustrate this to our linemen by explaining that the charge is similar to a racing dive into a swimming pool. They should be ready to explode as though triggered by a gun.

INDIVIDUAL ASSIGNMENTS FOR THE GAP EIGHT DEFENSE

Defensive ends: This assignment is the most difficult in the gap eight defense, as the defensive end must stop the most vulnerable area of penetration. He can be isolated by the offensive line blocking down and leaving him alone for a block by the on-side halfback (Diagram 59).

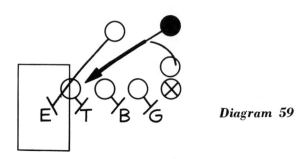

Diagram 59

The defensive end must be able to meet the kick-out block by the halfback and close the off-tackle hole. He must also be careful not to crack inside the halfback's block too hard, as the halfback will be able to hook him in, and the back carrying the ball will slide outside him. We want the defensive end to line up two feet outside the offensive end, angling in toward the quarterback. At the first movement of the end he will crack through the end's position from the outside in, down toward the quarterback, making sure to close the off-tackle hole. He must be prepared to meet the kick-out block of the halfback. His point of aim should be one yard behind where the quarterback lined up. At his initial charge, he should try to get a piece of the end as he cracks down toward the quarterback. If the flow of the play shows outside him, he should try to level off his charge, and force the play out wide so as not to put pressure on the defensive halfback, who has the sole responsibility of the outside. Defensive ends must stop the off-tackle play. If the play goes away from the end, he should chase the play as hard as possible into the backfield. If the play shows pass, he should continue his charge, altering it to be in position to maintain outside leverage on the quarterback. If the play shows

sprint-out pass to his side, he must alter his charge to the outside and contain the quarterback inside him. The quarterback
must not be able to sprint outside him (Diagram 60).

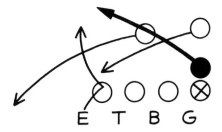

Diagram 60

Defensive tackles: The defensive tackle will line up in the
gap between the tackle and the end in a four-point stance.
He should be as low to the ground as possible, in a coiled
position ready to spring into the backfield. At the first movement of the hand of the offensive tackle or end, he will unleash
into the backfield in one motion trying to take a piece of the
offensive tackle with him. He must force for penetration, and
he must close the tackle gap, forcing the offensive tackle toward his own guard. Above all, he must force for penetration.
As soon as penetration is accomplished, he should look for legs
in the backfield, and grab as many as possible fighting towards
the action. The worst thing the defensive tackle could do would
be to remain on his own side of the line of scrimmage. If this
occurs, the men on either side of him become vulnerable, which
opens up an area to be run through (Diagram 61).

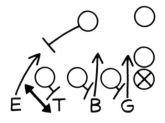

Diagram 61
Tackle Not Penetrating Opens Up
Too Large an Area for End to Close

Defensive guards: The defensive guards will line up in a four-point stance in the gap between the center and the guard. They should be low to the ground, coiled ready to explode into the backfield. At the first movement of the center's hand, the guards will explode right through the outer leg of the center, penetrating and pinching him into the backfield. They must drive as hard as they can, gaining penetration. They must drive through the center and get a piece of the quarterback's leg. They must stop the quarterback sneak and fullback up the middle cold. By cracking hard and taking a piece of the center's leg with them, they will cut off the possibility of the quick trap up the middle. Again, they must strive for penetration and get across the line of scrimmage. (See Diagram 62.)

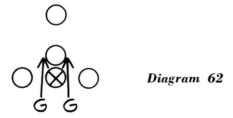

Diagram 62

Defensive linebackers: The defensive linebackers will line up in the four-point stance identical with that of the guards and tackles, in a coiled position between the offensive guard and tackle. The assignment is the same as that of the defensive tackle—penetration. At the first movement of the offensive guard, the linebackers will explode into the backfield, staying as low as possible and driving hard for penetration. They should try to close the gap, by cracking slightly more over the guard than over the tackle. They should try to force the guard into the center. As soon as they accomplish penetration, they should reach for as many backfield legs as they can find and try to cut off the quarterback's path. If the play shows pass, they should get up quickly and rush the passer as hard as they can. The defensive linebacker in this position can become vulnerable to a quick trap block coming from the offside guard. He must be prepared to meet this block and close hard. If he ever penetrates quickly without making contact with him, he should close hard to the inside expecting a trap block. (See Diagram 63.)

The charge of all eight defensive linemen, in the gap eight defense, is designed to give us one yard penetration into the backfield, where we can establish a defensive wall. (See Diagram 64.)

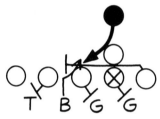

Diagram 63

Diagram 64

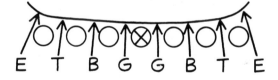

Play of the Defensive Secondary

Defensive Halfbacks: The defensive halfbacks will line up four yards deep, one yard outside the offensive end. They will read through the onside end into the backfield, and follow the flow of the backfield. They have definite outside responsibility and must come up exceedingly fast in order to contain a sweep. If the offensive end blocks in, they will fly up viciously to the outside. If the offensive end blocks out, they will come up quickly to the inside to help out on a play up the middle.

The defensive halfbacks have the responsibility of tackling any ballcarrier high from tackle to tackle, as the entire defensive line is working toward low penetration. They must be in position to stop a back leaping over the line. On any pass pattern, they will play zone pass defense most aggressively. They will take chances and gamble, and will play in front of any receiver. On an option play to their side, they must be in position to contain the pitch-out. They are not responsible for stopping the quarterback unless he crosses the line of scrimmage. The responsibility of stopping the quarterback on the option rests solely with the defensive end and middle safety.

If the ball is inside the five-yard line, the defensive halfback will line up two yards deep. He must realize that in this area there is no time for doubt. He must read their key and react immediately. If the flow of the play goes away from him, he must be aware of a possible bootleg by the quarterback, and must be in position to stop this (Diagram 65). He will be of little help in pursuing a play to the far side of the field on the goal line.

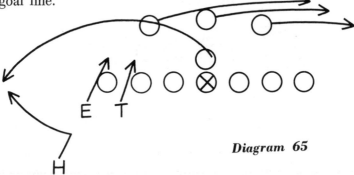

E   T

Diagram 65

H

Middle safety: The middle safety will line up three yards deep head on the center, and will read the flow of the backfield. His reaction will be determined by the flow of the backfield. He has no time to determine exactly what the play will be. He must move instinctively. If the play is coming up the middle, he must fire up and tackle high on the ballcarrier (Diagram 66). If the play is moving laterally, he must come up and cover the gap between the end and the defensive halfback. As he is moving laterally to protect the off-tackle hole, he should determine if the end on that side is releasing as a possible pass receiver. If he is, the safety will pick him up. If the play shows pass, he will cover the middle zone area, and read the eyes of the quarterback. He will be moving in the direction the quarterback looks and he may throw. He has no time to concern himself with receivers, but reacts to the quarterback.

The safety is responsible for meeting any ballcarrier head on from tackle to tackle on the line of scrimmage. All of his movements must become automatic, for he has no time to ponder a decision. As soon as the ball is snapped, he must be moving.

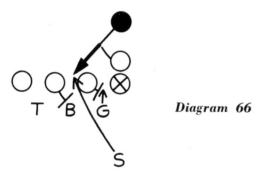

Diagram 66

ADJUSTMENTS IN THE GAP EIGHT DEFENSE

Adjustments for the gap eight are relatively simple. On the goal line the most important fact to remember is that aggressiveness is the only thing that will keep the other team from scoring. Therefore, all adjustments must be simple in order not to detract from this attitude of aggressiveness. We want only a few players to be aware of flankers or motion possibilities. The rest of the defense must concentrate completely on penetration.

The adjustments are as follows:

1. On a split end to either side, the defensive end will drop off and play inside the split end at a depth of four yards, and be responsible for him on pass coverage. The remainder of the defense will disregard the split end, and play the normal gap eight defense. The secondary will keep their responsibilities intact, and will not adjust to the split end (Diagram 67).

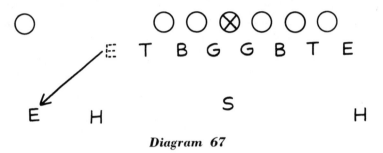

Diagram 67

2. On any back flankered to either side, the entire adjustment will be in the secondary. The halfback on the side of the flanker will be in position to cover the flanker-back. The remainder of the secondary will adjust slightly. The safety will move over two men to the side of the flanker to be in position to cover the tight end (Diagram 68).

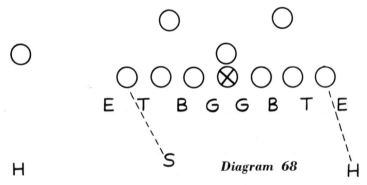

Diagram 68

3. On any type of motion, the adjustment again will be in the secondary. The defensive halfback to the side of the motion will have to pick up the motion man, and the remaining two secondary men will adjust as if it were a flanker-back (Diagram 69).

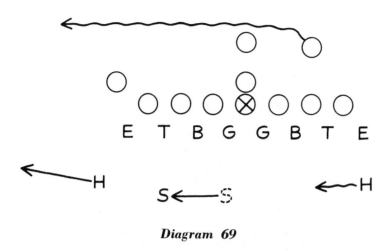

Diagram 69

4. On a split end and flanker, the rules remain constant. To the side of the split end, the defensive end on that side will drop off four yards and cover the split end. To the flanker-back side the halfback on that side will split out with him and cover him at a depth of four yards. The middle safety will move over two men towards the side of the remaining split end and will play normally from there (Diagram 70).

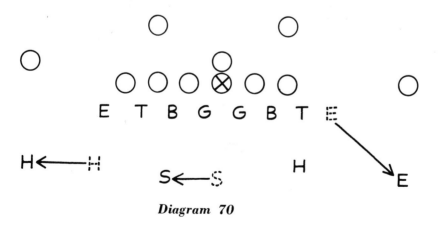

Diagram 70

*Northport defense (white jerseys) display savage gang tackling
to get to the ball carrier*

Northport linebacker Bob Leone gives 101 percent in blocking a punt

Skull and crossbones awards displayed on Northport helmet.
They are awarded for excellence in defensive play

Northport defensive end makes a determined effort to deflect a pass

*Northport defense (white jerseys) in determined pursuit to
get to the ball*

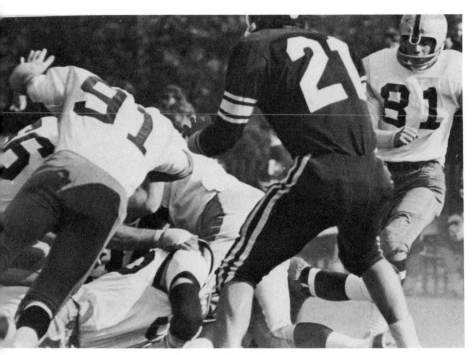

Northport (white jersey) gang tackling

Punt block

9

DEFENSIVE STRATEGY IN WINNING HIGH SCHOOL FOOTBALL

9

TRAIN YOUR SIGNAL CALLER

Spend as much time with your defensive signal caller as you do with your offensive signal caller. It is generally a simpler task to train your defensive signal caller, as there are fewer defenses than there are offensive plays. But a bad call by the defensive signal caller can be more disastrous than a bad call by your quarterback.

We train our defensive signal caller in two ways. The first way is on the blackboard. We diagram a field, giving the offensive field position, down distance, score, and quarterback tendencies. The defensive signal caller should know what defense to call and why. We use as many offensive situations as possible to give the defensive signal caller a variety of experiences. By working with the coach over a period of several weeks for about 15 minutes each day, the defensive quarterback can be adequately prepared to understand the reasons and thoughts for each defense to be called in any given situation. If the signal caller should make a bad defensive call on the blackboard, we carefully explain why it is a bad defensive call and what would have been a better call in that situation.

The second way to train the defensive quarterback is during defensive dummy scrimmage against the foreign team. In the defensive huddle, the coach gives the down distance and situation to the signal caller and he makes the appropriate call for the defense. Because we spend nearly 50 percent of our practice time on defense, much of that time is spent with our defensive unit going against the upcoming opponent's offense. We will go over every conceivable situation from third and very long yardage on the opponent's 40-yard line to fourth and three on the goal line.

The defensive signal caller, as the offensive quarterback, must learn to think exactly as the coach does. Under game conditions, he must be capable of reacting with poise and confidence and with a thorough knowledge and understanding of our total defensive philosophy. We feel that the defensive quarterback is more vital to our program than the offensive quarterback.

IF THEY HAVE TO SCORE, LET THEM SCORE IN THE AIR

To insure having an aggressive defensive unit, you must have the secondary commit quickly on sweeps and off-tackle plays. We believe firmly in teaching the reading of keys through repetition and immediate reaction thereafter. We want commitment now, with no hesitation. We explain to our secondary that once, possibly twice, during a season, we may get hit with a home run. But no team must score on the ground! Our defensive secondary is to be a firm part of the front containing unit. They must be able to read their keys quickly without hesitation on each play. We believe we will not lose often in the air; if a team is going to beat our defensive unit, it will have to grind out yardage on the ground. This is what we must stop first. We believe that if high school coaches would review the games lost over a period of several years, they would find that teams who beat them out-rushed them considerably. There will be exceptions to this, but, in our opinion, not too often. By emphasis on stopping the run first and then the pass, we would be quite happy to take a nine and one record each year. We feel that high school running teams are generally superior to passing teams. When we can stop the running game —if running is that team's strength—and make a team resort to its secondary method of moving the ball, the likelihood of their making a mistake becomes greater, and we will capitalize on it.

BLOCK THE PUNT, AND YOU WIN THE GAME

In keeping with our philosophy of defensive football, we believe it is more advantageous to block a punt than to return one for considerable yardage. The blocking of a punt is more demoralizing to a team than the returning of a punt, and much easier to do. Today, with progress being made in stressing punt coverage, there are fewer punt returns than there were five years ago. The vulnerability of high school players is more likely to be in the center and kicker positions, rather than in the line which would be covering punts. Consequently, most of our efforts are placed on the blocking of punts rather than on the return. Furthermore, we have found that by our consistently rushing the kicker, our opponents have reduced their coverage of the punt in expectation of the rush, resulting in extra yardage by our safeties in returning punts. We also strongly believe that anytime we block a punt, we will win the football game!

PRINCIPLES FOR BLOCKING A PUNT

To block a punt you must adhere to the following principles:

1. You must have a punt blocker. A boy with great courage and determination and no regard for his body is generally the best type. We usually like to put out a call for punt blockers and then give a number of them a try at it in live scrimmage. You cannot expect to block one in a game if you haven't practiced it successfully in a scrimmage.
2. You must free up your punt blocker. He must have a free shot at the kicker.
3. You must overload one of three areas: either side or the middle. The other areas must be left almost unguarded.

4. You must be reasonably certain that the opposition is going to punt.

THREE WINNING PUNT BLOCKS (Diagrams 69-71)

The following are three punt blocks that we have used successfully. You will notice that we are working completely to free up our punt blocker, and we always want to send him on a direct line.

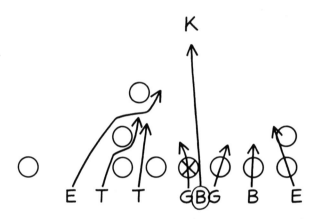

Diagram 71 (A)

PUNT BEFORE THE QUARTER,
WITH WIND AT YOUR BACK

We believe that one of the mistakes that high school coaches make is not to take advantage of a prevailing wind at the end of the quarter. When on your side of the fifty-yard line, as you approach any quarter, you should punt on the second or the third down when there is just enough time to run another play or two. You should give up a possible first down to get the punt off with a strong wind behind you. Many times, this will

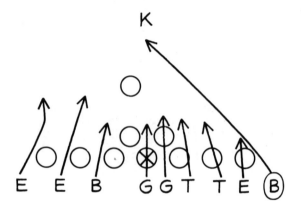

Diagram 71 (B)

result in a thirty-yard difference in exchange of punts by your team, punting with the wind and then turning around to have the wind in your face. Too many times a team will try to make their first down, and will refuse to punt on the second or third down, even though the distance on the punt gained might be double the punt tried with the wind in your face. If necessary, you should also call a time out just before the end of the quarter so as to insure getting your punting team into the ball game. It will always be worth the time out to have this advantage.

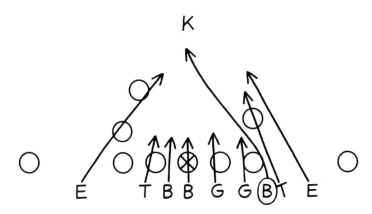

Diagram 71 (C)

Too many times I have seen a team wait until fourth down to punt as the quarter changes, and then have to punt with a strong wind in their face. This is a great discouragement to the average high school punter, who should be given every opportunity to punt with the wind in his favor. There is also the advantage of punting on second or third down when the defensive team does not expect it, will not set up a block or a return, and can not possibly receive it adequately. I have seen average high school punters kicking with the wind in their face averaging 20 or 25 yards, but, kicking with the wind at their back, 50 or 60 yards. It is a great advantage, and one that should not be neglected.

HOPE YOU LOSE THE TOSS OF THE COIN

We believe strongly that it is a great advantage to kick off rather than to receive the opening kickoff. Our football team is emotionally ready to play ball at kickoff. They are in a savage state and are ready for brutal contact, rather than for the finesse required to return the kickoff. Hence, we always want to kick off if there is any wind advantage at all. This factor works in reverse as well; the team receiving the kickoff is in a nervous state and may fumble the kickoff or make a mistake. And a mistake here will usually result in a touchdown and possible change of the outcome.

We at Northport have kicked off almost every game for the past four years. We send our captains out for the toss with instructions to take the goal with the wind at our backs. If we win the toss, we will defend that goal, and usually our opponents elect to receive. However, we hope to lose the toss, and that our opponent will elect to receive, giving us the choice of goals or choice of second half kickoff. If we are winning or in a tie ball game at halftime, we again elect to defend the goal with the wind at our backs. If we are behind at halftime, we may elect to receive (assuming we lost the pre-game), as possession of the ball then becomes paramount.

It is also important to develop a strong kickoff man capable of putting the ball into the end zone or as close to it as possible. It is always difficult to begin a football game with the ball on your own 20, and against a keyed up defensive unit, particularly if your offense is tight or unsure. The first five minutes of most high school games will often produce offensive mistakes, and these can be the breaks of the game for the defense.

MOMENTUM IS EVERYTHING

Momentum plays a large part in any football season. A team winning a number of games in succession moves like a steamroller with a force at its back. This force is momentum. With momentum on your side, each individual ballplayer, as an integral part of a team unit, plays to the greatest capacity of his ability. He has a feeling of running downhill. The smart coach will capitalize on this feeling, and help to build up momentum.

Momentum is the reason a team will score quickly after recovering a fumble, blocking a punt, intercepting a pass, or after any break occurring in the opposition's half of the field. The team will perhaps capitalize on momentum again on the first play from scrimmage with a long pass or an end run that goes all the way. This team has momentum; the other team has lost it.

When your team is moving the ball continuously and successfully, the plays should be run quickly, with no time-outs to halt this momentum. Pressure must be placed on the opposition by continually pounding its weaknesses. Very conservative plays should be used involving a minimum of ball handling and the least possibility of error. Momentum itself will help to move the ball.

HOW TO KEEP MOMENTUM GOING

To keep momentum going, your team must:

1. Have more enthusiasm than their opponents.
2. Line up and break from their huddle sharply and quickly.
3. Use very simple plays.
4. Make absolutely no mistakes.
5. Have no penalties.
6. Run plays over opponent's substitutes.
7. Come back with a counter-off, a very strong running play after it has been run successfully a number of times.
8. Make any passes short ones that will, based on percentages, have the greatest chance for completion.
9. Be fiercely aggressive.
10. Have the attitude of complete confidence in every team member.
11. Display great enthusiasm on the bench at all times.
12. Have complete confidence in their ability to score— *but not be in a hurry to score.*

HOW TO STOP MOMENTUM AGAINST YOU

Now the question arises, if the opposition has momentum what can you do to combat it? We have found that the easiest and quickest way to stop a team's momentum when they are moving the ball well against you is to call time out. This simple piece of strategy has been used frequently by basketball coaches for the same purpose, but has been neglected on the football field. If the defensive team is being run over by the offense and consistent yardage is ground out over them play after play, the need for renewed enthusiasm and organization is evident. By the simple act of calling a time out, the team has a chance to regroup, to talk over the problem, to determine where the offense is running and how they are moving the ball. It gives the captains a chance to speak to the players and to boost their enthusiasm, and it gives the coach the opportunity to send in adjustments and to make substitutions of players who may inspire the team.

The time out may also result in a quieting down of the offensive unit. It becomes a cooling off period for them, while the defense, when given a chance to talk things over among themselves, will come back fired up. There has been too much talk about saving your time outs until just before the half for a scoring drive. High school teams are not proficient at moving the ball with two minutes remaining in the half and the time outs may be utilized to much greater advantage by spacing them out where they are most needed for discussion and renewed enthusiasm.

During a ball game when the opposition is moving the ball well and the defense has not been able to stop it, the high school football player believes that someone else along the line is not doing his job. By calling time out, the entire defensive line and linebackers can correct errors in alignment and get a psychological lift from feeling that they have corrected an apparent weakness.

DO NOT GAMBLE DEFENSIVELY AND CALL A GAP
OR GOAL LINE DEFENSE

Reading through these pages you probably have realized that we, at Northport, play very conservative football. Our concept of good high school football is to play defense, hit hard and pursue. We try to eliminate any possible mistake. We feel that to gamble on a short-yardage situation on any part of the field, with the exception of inside the ten-yard line with a goal line defense is a grave mistake. We would prefer, on a third and one, to play a normal defense and give the opposition the first down if we cannot stop them with a basic defense. First downs do not score points. Too many times a long gainer or touchdown may result when a team jumps into a goal line defense on a short-yardage situation and fails to cover all areas of the field adequately. Yet there are a few situations throughout a season or a game when it pays to go into a gap or goal line defense. These particular situations should be memorized by every member of the team so that if they should arise, in the heat and emotion of a game, the players would instinctively know how to react.

SITUATIONS CALLING FOR A
GOAL LINE DEFENSE

The specific situations where we will go into a goal line defense other than on the goal line are as follows:

1. *Never,* if we are ahead by more than eight points.
2. *Never,* if we are behind by less than seven points.
3. If we are behind by more than seven points.
4. If we are positive, through scouting, that a specific play will be run in short (yardage) situation, and it is the first time it has occurred in the game. We must be confident of what the play will be and who will carry the ball. Once we have done this for the first time and have stopped the play, we are reluctant to do it again.
5. To stop momentum. After a team has ground out three or four first downs on us, and the situation seems crucial, we will then jump into a goal line defense on a fourth or third down and short yardage.
6. In a very rare situation, when our opponents are passing and continually eating up yardage, and we cannot gain a good pass rush with our normal defenses, we will call a goal line defense in anticipation of the pass and of getting a good rush.

These are the only situations where we may use the goal line defense other than inside the ten-yard line. When we do use it, we must be fairly confident of the opposition's call on the next play from scrimmage. If there is doubt, the goal line or gap defense will never be called.

THE IMPORTANCE OF FIELD POSITION

Field position is a vital factor in high school defensive football. This must be kept in mind at all times. All defensive football revolves around field position. As I have previously stated, the objective of the defensive unit is to get the offensive team the ball inside their opponent's territory within scoring range. Conversely, the object of the offensive team is to move the ball outside their own territory (for example, get off a successful punt), so that the defensive team will be in position to force a break and gain possession of the ball for the offense to score!

With this in mind, field position boils down to this: *Keep the football away from our own goal line and move in position to be as close to the goal line of our opposition.* This is the most important single aspect which will determine the eventual winner of a close contest. Many high school football coaches take field position for granted, assuming it is beyond their ability to change in the normal outcome of a football game. We do not believe this. We believe you must plan for field position. You must teach sound theories to the entire squad so that they thoroughly understand the philosophy behind them.

To teach proper field position theory you must first establish the basic assumption that your team is a strong defensive unit, and further, that no long run or pass play will develop against you for a touchdown. Each member of the team must believe in this. We realize that in the course of a football season that this will occur; a long run or pass will result in one or two touchdowns against us. But we indoctrinate our team with the thought that when this does occur, we ourselves will make the long run or pass for a touchdown to counterbalance it. Therefore, if we can assume that the long run and pass occurring throughout a season will work for the opposition as well as ourselves, we can discount this and work solely for development of field position as our main objective.

There are specific objectives we teach in the classroom and on the field about field position. This is a mental preparation to offset seeming to be over-conservative at times.

The following list contains significant factors in determining field position, and how to insure good field position:

HOW TO INSURE GOOD FIELD POSITION

1. We must keep the ball in the opposition's half of the field in hopes of forcing a mistake.

2. Our offense must be geared to get us in a position to punt if we can't score. When we are deep in our part of the field, our offense must grind out one or two first downs without making a mistake and successfully get off a punt to put the ball back into our opponent's territory.

3. We must never gamble for a first down on the fourth down. Even the successful gamble may not affect the score, and if you do not make the first down on the gamble, there is the chance your opponents may score. Also, if you punt rather than go for the first down at, say, about midfield, the ball is received at about the 15, making it possible for an error to give you possession. We never gamble for a first down.

4. We must pick up the hidden yards. A team passing unsuccessfully from its own 30-yard line in three successive downs, will be in poor field position to punt: If they started on their 30, then after three unsuccessful passes they would be punting from approximately their own 18-yard line. If the passer was thrown for a loss on one try, they then could be punting from their own 14-yard line.

However, a hard-nosed running offensive team, unsuccessful in a first down attempt starting on their 30-yard line, would probably average two or three yards per carry. This would put them on about the 36- to 39-yard line with fourth down in the punt situation, and they would be punting from about the 28 or 30 as opposed to an unsuccessful passing team punting from about the 14- to 18-yard line. The net gain to the running team is about 12 to 15 yards if both punters are about equal. If both teams are strong defensively, and this occurs on three or four consecutive series of plays for each team, the running team (assuming they would only average a below-minimum two and a half yards per carry) would gain nearly 40 yards on four exchanges of the football, thus placing them in four-down territory with a definite advantage.

We must constantly move the ball even when a particular play is unsuccessful. One further point—a passing team having thrown two unsuccessful passes on a third and ten, is far more likely to make a mistake resulting in interception or a break for the other team, than the team who has run the first two downs and has averaged two or three yards with a third and four situation. We strongly believe that a running team will always have a better field position than the passing team, assuming that both teams are relatively equal.

5. We must handle punts! All coaches fear the dropped punt in their own territory. To insure field position, high school coaches must teach and prepare the handling of punts by the safety men. Nothing is so devastating as a punt bouncing down the field and rolling dead on your own five-yard line, when it could have been handled on the 25-yard line! This must be drilled and constantly practiced. Big losses in field position generally occur when the safeties are not prepared to handle the punt. Catching punts is a must, unless there is a large chance of error.

6. You must cover punts. A team not covering a punt loses valuable yardage by the other team running back a punt. We tell our team that punt formation is the most important formation we have in our entire offense. We *never* want a runback of more than three or four yards. We feel that you must work and practice for this. The team must believe that

this is a vital offensive play, that we can stop cold any punt return.

7. Always be moving the ball forward. This sounds fairly obvious, since we all want to move the ball forward all the time. But by this we mean to eliminate all plays in your offense which have a possibility of resulting in a loss. This would include plays such as the wide reverse, which sometimes may result in an eight- to ten-yard loss; a delayed draw play, where the fullback may be caught deep in his backfield; or too much of a delayed sweep, where a containment man may catch the halfback four or five yards in his own backfield. Every play in your offense must be geared to cross that line of scrimmage. If it does not, it will hurt your field position, and must be eliminated.

8. You must reduce penalties to a minimum. Penalties are a major breakdown in field position. Certain penalties will occur and there isn't a great deal to be done about them. However, many penalties you can coach to eliminate. There is never an excuse for clipping. If your team is aware of this, a coach can stop an intrasquad game when he sees a clip to reprimand the guilty player. A coaching staff that emphasizes the correction of penalties during practice and coaches against them, will have a minimum of penalties in a ballgame. *Coach against penalties.*

10

HOW TO SELECT PERSONNEL
FOR A WINNING
DEFENSIVE SYSTEM

At Northport, our defensive coaching is broken down into three units. Each coach is assigned one unit; that unit works independently of the other two; then all three are coordinated into a cohesive defensive unit. These three units are:

1. Defensive Secondary: consists of three positions—left halfback, safety and right halfback.
2. Linebackers and Ends: consists of four positions—left and right defensive ends and left and right linebackers.
3. Defensive Line: consists of four positions on the defensive line—left tackle, right tackle, left guard, and right guard.

The placing of personnel in proper positions is a difficult and vital task which we try to undertake in the spring. To do this we list all our returning lettermen from the varsity, all of the junior varsity players, and those freshmen who have shown promise on a master list. The staff places each name in one of the above units.

The defensive positions listed in order of importance are:

1. safety
2. left linebacker
3. left defensive end
4. right linebacker
5. left halfback
6. right defensive end
7. left tackle
8. left guard

9. right halfback
10. right tackle
11. right guard

Now, the problem is to place those athletes with superior ability at the top of this list. Of course experience, physical stature, and desire to play the game must be taken into consideration. Note, then, that our safety will be our best all-around football player, and our strongest boys will play on the left defensive side. Through past experience we have learned that our opponents will generally be right-handed football teams, and will run and throw mostly going to their right.

SAFETY

Strongest and best football player, senior, over six feet in height. Most of our safeties have, in the past, been over 6'2" with the exception of one boy who was 5'9" and a superior athlete. The safety must love contact and have natural athletic ability with good eye-hand coordination. He must have good speed and quick reactions, and must be able to diagnose plays and react accordingly as well as learn to read keys. Our safety usually has the most tackles and part tackles in a given season. He must be aggressive, able to fly up to the line of scrimmage to make tackles, or retreat back to cover the long pass. He must have a burning desire to play football. He must also be a leader. In many instances our safety has also been our quarterback. He should be highly respected by members of the team. As I have mentioned, our safety is our most valuable football player; if he lacks the above-mentioned characteristics we will have little chance of winning a championship, but if he is an excellent safety he will compensate for other teammates with less ability.

LEFT LINEBACKER

Must be strong, quick and of adequate size, preferably tall and lanky. We have used boys from 160 pounds on up in this position. He must have a great desire for physical contact, an exceptional ability to tackle, and good lateral speed. He must be able to cross-key and diagnose plays rapidly. He is a part of the pass defense and should be able to play the long pass and be an aggressive defender to stop the running game. He must be steady so as not to react improperly to his keys, and he must have a fierce competitive desire to win. This position always calls for one of our most experienced players. Our left linebacker should be an intelligent savage!

LEFT DEFENSIVE END

Should be tall, close to 200 pounds, have good agility and eye-hand coordination. He should be a good athlete, not necessarily highly-experienced, but intelligent and competitive. He must be strong enough to close the off-tackle hole and meet drive blocking by the fullback. He must be tough and durable, with good upper arm strength, and good speed. He must also have good eyesight. This is a difficult position unless the individual has height and size to withstand punishment.

RIGHT LINEBACKER

Our fourth most important position must cover the entire right side of the line and make tackles on the left side as well. Therefore, he must have good strength, speed and adequate size. He should be intelligent and have the ability to react and tackle. We would like him to be as close in ability as possible to our left linebacker. We try to find an underclassman with the capabilities and talent to fill the shoes of our safety or left linebacker the following year.

LEFT DEFENSIVE HALFBACK

Generally must have varsity experience lettering the previous year in the secondary. Must have good speed, average size, and good eye-hand coordination and agility. He should be self-confident, hard-working and determined. He does not have to have great talent. He must, however, be capable of reading keys of the end, tackle and halfback without watching the quarterback. He must be cool under pressure with the ability to come up quickly on sweeps, to play the long pass, and to tackle on the opposite side of the field in pursuit. He must be aggressive and poised. We have always used a senior in this position.

RIGHT DEFENSIVE END

Sixth most important position must be of good size, preferably over 6'1" and close to 200 pounds. He must be strong and have good arms. He must have the ability to tackle and to meet the blocks of the pulling guards, and to close the off-tackle hole. He should be intelligent and dedicated. We generally like in this position an underclassman who would be capable of playing left defensive end or linebacker in his senior year. His speed may be average, but he must have quick reactions. It is very difficult to play a small boy in this position, as he must be strong enough to maintain his ground, deliver a blow, fight the interference and force the play inside or make the tackle himself. He also must be able to move laterally.

LEFT DEFENSIVE TACKLE

Our strong side tackle should be of good size. He is usually one of our biggest linemen. He must possess a great desire to play and win. He must have the ability to hit and crack down; he must like contact. We would like a boy with good speed, but this can be compensated for if he can hustle and give 101 percent effort all the time. This position is a difficult, brutal position which demands great strength and the ability to take great punishment. It is a job which offers little reward, because play after play the left tackle is eating dirt and cracking down hard, protecting our linebacker. He must take punishment from the end blocking down on him, the tackle firing out

at him, the halfback drive blocking at him, and the guards pulling and trapping on him. So you can se. that the position requires strength, size, desire to play, ability to react and the
ability to pursue. Of our four defensive linemen this position
is the most important. It is also difficult because he must play
opposite the opponent's best lineman, and must not be intimi-
dated by him.

LEFT DEFENSIVE GUARD

This position requires a very quick individual, one who is
strong enough to ward off the block of the offensive guard, and
. ble to move laterally. We feel we can use any size boy in this
position, providing he has the strength at least to maintain a
stalemate with the offensive guard. Primarily he'll be moving
laterally, so quickness must be paramount over strength. In
the past we have found a boy who is tall, preferably over 6
feet, and weighing 175 to 190, with quick lateral movement
to be the best candidate for this position. We have used boys
who have been linebackers in junior high or JV play, but who
are not good enough to be starting linebackers in varsity play,
and found them to be outstanding. It is difficult to use a very
big boy in this position even though he is very strong, if he
does not have unusual lateral mobility. Being tall helps in
this position in defending against the pass. The coach must
be careful placing a boy in this position, not to sacrifice speed
for size.

RIGHT DEFENSIVE HALFBACK

This is the weakest position in our defensive secondary and
requires an athlete of outstanding ability, good size, decent
speed, and good hand-eye coordination. Although our left
defensive halfback is the more important position, the right
halfback still must have outside responsibility for the running
game, must be capable of coming up and tackling quickly on
sweeps, and must defend against the forward pass. Again,

we like a boy in this position to be an underclassman with promising athletic ability, in order to gear him for a possible left defensive halfback or safety in the future.

RIGHT DEFENSIVE TACKLE

Must be strong, with good size and quick lateral movement. He must be able to take punishment, to react to the block of the defensive end, and to spin out to pursue the outside play. He must also be capable of pursuit to the strong side of the field. This position is good training for a potential tackle or junior lineman who has seen action as a sophomore but hasn't reached complete physical growth as yet. The normal progression would be for this position to become left defensive tackle the following year. We prefer a boy with fairly good size, but have used a small boy who was extremely aggressive. He must be able to take punishment and contact on every single play, so strength is important. This position does not demand great intelligence, as most of the reactions can be learned from repetitious drill. It is a good position for a boy who enjoys constant physical contact and the heat of battle.

RIGHT DEFENSIVE GUARD

Must have strength and good lateral speed; should be aggressive and able to react quickly. Intelligence helps! Must be capable of rushing the passer. In past years we have played in this position a very light boy (about 160 pounds), who was aggressive and had great desire to play football but lacked the physical stature to play another line position. To play a larger but slower boy in this position is a mistake, as it requires lateral movement rather than just protecting an area.

As you can see our most experienced players are placed in the top five positions, and those with less experience generally fill in the remaining positions. The less experienced players are capable athletes who will be able to fill those top five positions in following years. We tell our defensive team that our defense is only as good as its weakest link, so we cannot have a patsy in any position! By selecting carefully, knowing our personnel, and measuring the characteristics of each player along these guidelines, we can achieve successful placement.

11

HOW TO GET YOUR TEAM READY MENTALLY FOR A WINNING DEFENSE

To have your team ready to play a vicious contact game of rock-ribbed gang tackling and great pursuit, a game that by the sheer nature of it will probably produce injury to your opponents or yourselves, a team must be completely prepared mentally and emotionally to do battle at game time. High school teams that are not ignited into a feverish psychological pitch at game time are at a great disadvantage, and will probably lose.

If two teams are approximately equal in ability and have had the benefit of sound coaching, we feel strongly that the team mentally prepared at game time will be victorious. This may also work in reverse. If both teams are equally prepared mentally to play one another, then one will nullify the other and additional factors will enter into the outcome such as personnel, coaching, officiating, the bounce of the football, etc. However, if the players on one team are not keyed up, they are in for a long afternoon of football. If high school football players are to hit with a passion, and pursue recklessly, they must be mentally ready to play football.

PLAY EACH GAME AS IF IT WERE
A SEASON IN ITSELF

We want our football teams to look at each game we play as if it were a complete season in itself. All our practice time, all our working team, all our related thoughts throughout the week are geared toward our imminent opponent. There is never a mention of a later-season ball game, or a thought f anything beyond this next game. We want each game that we play to be a complete entity in itself, and we want to feel that nothing exists after this impending game. For us, this is our whole season, this game only. All we do the preceding week is a countdown to game time. Each game must be built up as the most important game thus far. We must be unmoved by all outside factors and stimuli and concentrate only on the one objective in our minds. Throughout the week, we are slowly building up great pressure towards the Saturday game. By Saturday morning, we want the pressure to be almost explosive on each member of the team. We never want to reduce pressure, only to increase it.

21 HOURS TO KICKOFF

We maintain a set procedure during the 21 hours preceding kickoff. We have used this procedure for four years and find it most successful for us. It goes something like this:

Friday, 5:00 P.M. We have finished our last practice, normally a light one, in our game uniforms. After showering and dressing, the team goes home for dinner.

8:00 Our weekly Friday night meeting is held in our football room. We are extremely fortunate to have a room ideally suited for our purposes. It is a small theater-shaped room containing about 80 seats, with a platform in front, surrounded by blackboards. The room has no windows to distract us. In the back is a projection room, which we use for game films. The meeting normally lasts about one hour. The normal format includes a lecture by the head coach about our Saturday opponent. A general description of the philosophy and personality of the opponent is stressed, leading to the individual tendencies of each formation we will face, the defenses we will meet, and any unusual type of play we can expect. At this time, we will sick the team on the opponent's chief personnel, normally their scorer. This procedure is described in Chapter 3.

Although the team has reviewed the opponent's offensive and defensive formations continually, during the entire week of practice sessions and lectures, for some reason they will have a thousand questions! They are keyed up for the game, and all the questions they may not have asked during the week will be brought out in the last twenty minutes of a question and answer period. The meeting is usually terminated by a few last remarks by the head coach on what this game means to the team and how important it is. After the meeting, the team members are free to do as they please, as long as they are in bed by 11:00.

Saturday, 9:30 A.M.   The team reports to the football locker room. Here each player will lay out his equipment and uniform in front of his own locker, and make sure everything is in perfect condition. During the next hour, the team is left alone and there is generally very little talk.

10:25   The captains get the squad lined up and report to the coaches that the team is ready for their pre-game meal. They then march through the school to the faculty dining room which is used for the pre-game meal. The dining room, which has been previously arranged to contain the exact number of tables and seats for the entire squad, coaching staff and managers, allows no one else in while the team is eating.

It has become tradition that during the pre-game meal there will be no conversation. Each member of the team goes about the business of eating his meal if he can. As soon as a boy has finished eating and returned his tray, he waits for the entire team to finish. When everyone has finished, the captains will signal the coach that the team is ready to be dismissed. The team is dismissed and must be back in the locker by 11:55. Their time is now their own.

Most of the boys are happy to get out of the dining room, as the mounting tension and silence become almost unbearable. Many of the boys go to church; some go to one of the junior high school games played on Saturday morning; and some go into the football locker room and just sit there for their free hour. The point here is that each boy is entitled to spend the time as he wishes.

11:55 The team reports back to the football locker room, where the taping procedure begins. Our line coach tapes all linemen from tackle to tackle, and the backfield coach tapes the entire backfield and the ends. The taping is done by seniority; captain is taped first, senior lettermen, then junior lettermen, and so forth. As soon as a boy is finished being taped, he begins to dress in his game suit. When he finishes dressing, he walks through the football locker room into the gymnasium, where mats have been laid out. Each boy lies down to relax until called. There is a manager stationed there and if any equipment, tape or the like is needed, the manager will send to the coach's office for it. The taping is generally completed by 12:25, and dressing by 12:50. The remainder of the pre-game period is spent lying on the mats, giving each ball player a chance to rest with his own thoughts. The gym is in semi-darkness, and there is absolutely no conversation, with the exception of a check on an assignment or specific play, or defensive key. We like to have the team resting on the mats for at least half an hour before our pre-game warm-up.

1:00 We like to spend time with the defensive quarterback going over goal line situations, discussing when to call the goal line defense and when to jump out of it. A bad call on the goal line will almost always cost you a touchdown.

1:25 The captains are called into the coach's office, and given their options on the toss and any last minute instructions necessary.

1:30 The team is led out onto the field by the captains for the pre-game warm-up. The backfield and line coaches will go out with the team for the warm-up; the head coach will not.

1:45 The team comes back into the football locker room and each boy sits in front of his own locker. The captains are then sent out for the toss of the coin.

1:52   The coaching staff enters the locker room to address the team. The captains have returned by this time.

1:55   The team all kneels in a huddle for a minute of silence. Then the captains lead the team out onto the playing field.

The team is now mentally ready to play football. They have been eating, talking, drinking and thinking football since 9:30 A.M. This is a solid four and a half hours of concentration before game time. We firmly believe that it is impossible to have a team come in at noon and be mentally ready to play football by 2:00. It requires great mental preparation, with constant dedication to detail. The team that is not completely ready emotionally to play football at game time is at a great disadvantage.

LET THEM SWEAT AT HOME

This is certainly not a new idea. A few years ago we began this procedure, and we feel it has great merit. It has been good to us for the last few years. We are certain that it has contributed in some way to the fact that we have scored first in most of our games over the past four years. Considering the psychological nature of the high school athlete, we believe that this procedure has given us a slight mental advantage at game time. We will take any legal advantage that we can get all the time!

By "let them sweat," we mean not letting our opponent see our team until two minutes before game time. We use a practice field on the other side of the school for our warm-up. It is impossible for the opposition to see us warming up. They, of course, must warm up in the stadium or the adjoining practice field. The first intimation that there is an opponent comes at the toss of the coin at 1:45. The entire team does not enter the stadium until two minutes of 2:00.

We believe that this small maneuver can shake up our opposition, and even unnerve them. While they warm up, they may be watching for us, waiting for our entrance. One team even went so far as to skip a warm-up session, in order not to miss our entrance. This seems to point to a psychological advantage we may possibly hold.

12

HOW TO SCOUT FOR
DEFENSIVE FOOTBALL

Scouting, even on the high school level, has now become a science. To play top defensive football week after week, you must have a solid, well-organized scouting program. In the present-day era of high school football, just about every team scouts the opposition. The questions arise; how good is each returned scouting report, how well is it interpreted, and how well is it communicated to the players?

On this last point, all scouting is completely useless unless it is communicated to the players. Too many coaches absorb a scouting report completely, and know the opposition thoroughly, yet cannot communicate it to their players.

WHAT DO WE WANT TO KNOW FROM A SCOUTING REPORT?

1. Where they run
   a. What kind of plays
   b. How frequently
   c. Who carries the ball
   d. Is there a particular down where a play is called
   e. From which particular side of the field

2. How they pass
   a. Ability of quarterback
   b. Ability of ends
   c. Ability of halfback receivers
   d. Type and ability of pass protection
   e. Ability of quarterback to run when setting to pass
   f. What are the patterns, including screen and draw

3. How is their kicking game
   a. What type of punt formation
   b. How quickly does the punter get off the ball
   c. How good is the protection
   d. How good is the coverage
   e. How good is the snap from center

4. How is their kick-off game
   a. Distance of kicker
   b. How do they cover it? Do receivers cross
   c. Is there a safety man
   d. Who gets down quickly
   e. Where should we return the kick

5. How do they return kick-offs
   a. Any very fast receivers
   b. What type of returns do they use

All of the above information must be known. Therefore, our scouting must revolve around the principle that everything brought back on a scouting report must be complete and usable. After the coaching staff is well-versed on the information brought back by the scout, we break it down in its simplest form to the players. We want to communicate *these three essential tasks to the team:*

1. What three plays do we have to stop?
2. Which individuals do we have to stop?
3. What must we do to win the game?

HOW TO ORGANIZE YOUR SCOUTING PROGRAM

1. Set up your scouting forms and procedures. Have them dittoed and have them available. The scouting forms which we use will be detailed in this chapter.

2. Appoint three or four scouts who are available for the season. We do not believe in using assistant varsity coaches, as they have definite assignments on game day and are needed on the field. We use our junior varsity coaches and freshmen coaches. In the past, we have also trained interested local people who have played football for Northport, or who have a fine football background and are interested in scouting. Anyone with a good background and understanding of football, we believe, can be trained to do an adequate job of scouting.

3. Have your scouting assignments dittoed and the entire schedule set at least two weeks before the opening game. Each scout must know well in advance what games he will scout, the dates and the time. The scouting schedule should be worked out so as not to rush a scout, so he will have plenty of time to get there well in advance, and be relaxed enough to concentrate.

4. Get pay for your scouts. Most people who are scouting for you are dedicated to the game of football, and really do not need any compensation for a good scouting job. But we have found that if you can give them a few dollars for expenses, gas, perhaps lunch, you can expect a better job, and will find little or no resistance to scouting chores. We give our scouts ten dollars per game, which is merely a token amount, but we feel it helps. Suggested ways of obtaining this money are through budgeting, through your local booster club, or pulling it from gate receipts. It doesn't amount to a great deal of money throughout the season, and it is very important that the scouts be paid for each scouting job.

5. Set up a time on the day after the game is scouted for the coach to meet with the scout. The scouting report must be completed at this time. We have found that the best procedure is for the scout to give his report to the head coach alone, and for him, in turn, to interpret it to his staff. If the scouting procedure is well organized and the forms comprehensive, the entire meeting of the coach and the scout takes no more than 30 minutes.

6. Have the scouting schedule set up so that all opponents are scouted at least twice before you play them, and three times if possible. If you can scout them only twice, send your

best scout out last. If you are going to scout them three times, then it is permissible to have one scout see them twice and the other see them once.

7. Have staff meetings every Sunday night to go over and accumulate information from the scouting reports. This procedure should become routine, whether you win or lose.

8. Give recognition to scouts whenever possible.

9. Have all terms and the names given the formations and different sets standardized so that communication between the scouts and the coaching staff is consistent. A list should be drawn up and distributed throughout the coaching staff, from seventh grade on up and to all scouts. Once everyone becomes familiar with the terms and learns to use them fluently, a great deal of time is saved and communication without error becomes much simpler. When referring to specific plays of the opposition, we use our own numbering system for a comparative play in our offense. A list of formations and the describing terms are noted in Diagram 72.

INDIVIDUAL PLAY CHART

The first scouting chart that we use is our individual play chart as illustrated in Diagrams 73 and 74. Each page is divided into four individual play charts. This is the scout's work sheet, and is the only type of sheet the scout has with him at the game itself. The scout will carry approximately 30 of these work sheets with him in a loose-leaf notebook. All information dealing with the ball game will be noted on these pages. Each sheet will contain one series of downs or four plays. If a series contains only two plays (i.e., a fumble or interception on the second down), only those two plays appear on the one page, and the sheet is turned over for the next series of downs. The same holds true if the team makes a first down on the second play; the page will have only those two plays.

The top of each play chart is self-explanatory. The first column on top, which is completely filled out before the play

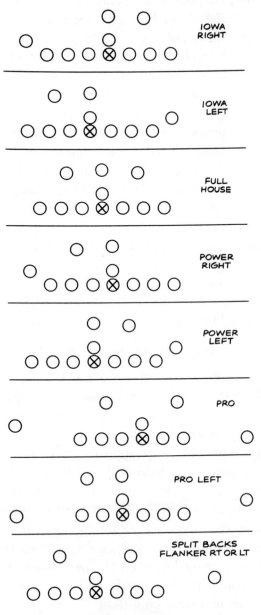

Diagram 72
Formation Terminology

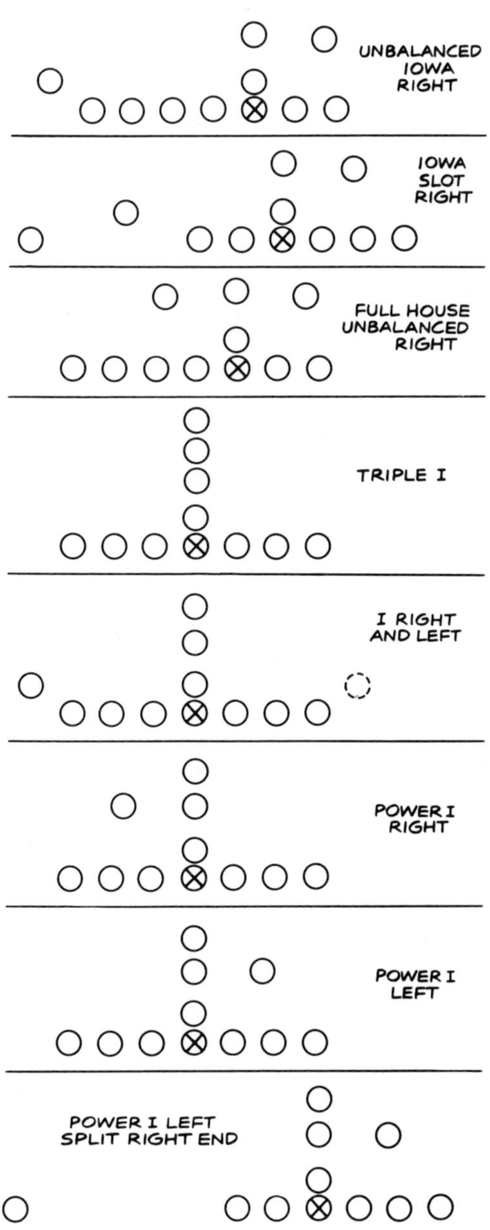

UNBALANCED
IOWA
RIGHT

IOWA
SLOT
RIGHT

FULL HOUSE
UNBALANCED
RIGHT

TRIPLE I

I RIGHT
AND LEFT

POWER I
RIGHT

POWER I
LEFT

POWER I LEFT
SPLIT RIGHT END

Diagram 72 (cont'd.)

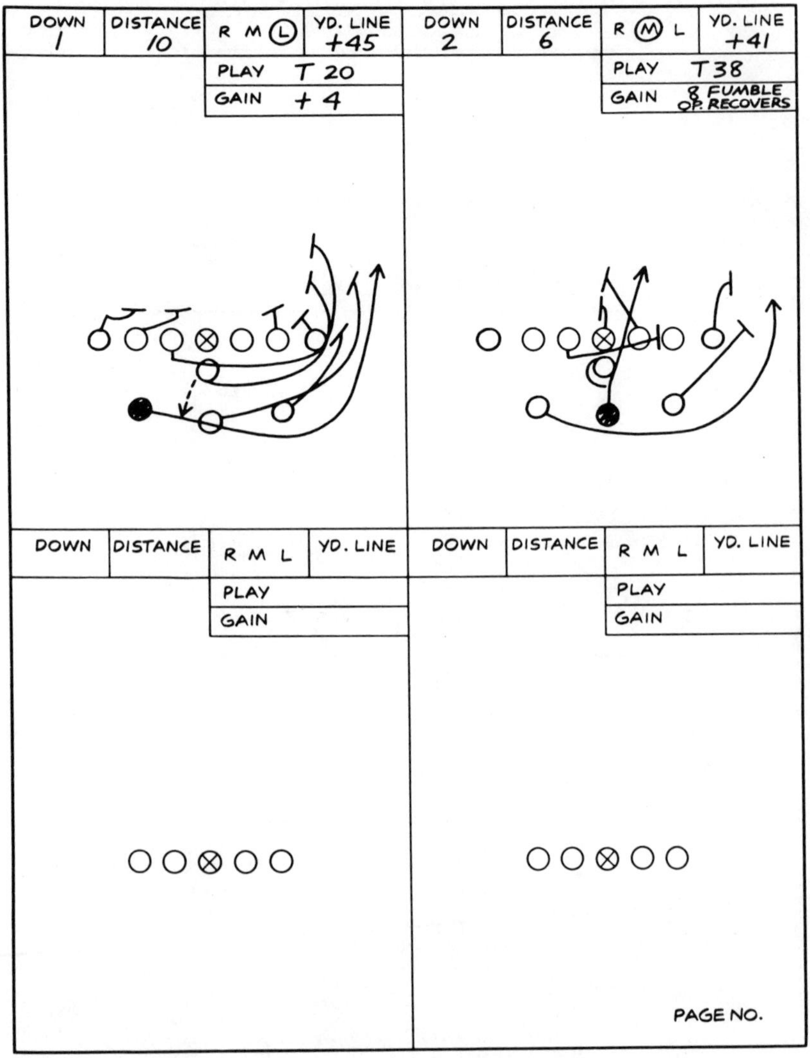

DOWN 1	DISTANCE 10	R M Ⓛ	YD. LINE +45	DOWN 2	DISTANCE 6	R Ⓜ L	YD. LINE +41
		PLAY	T 20			PLAY	T 38
		GAIN	+ 4			GAIN	8 FUMBLE OP. RECOVERS

DOWN	DISTANCE	R M L	YD. LINE	DOWN	DISTANCE	R M L	YD. LINE
		PLAY				PLAY	
		GAIN				GAIN	

PAGE NO.

Diagram 73

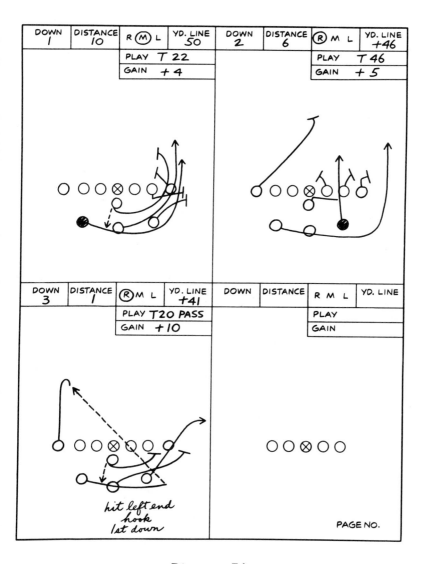

DOWN 1	DISTANCE 10	R Ⓜ L	YD. LINE 50
	PLAY	T 22	
	GAIN	+ 4	

DOWN 2	DISTANCE 6	Ⓡ M L	YD. LINE +46
	PLAY	T 46	
	GAIN	+ 5	

DOWN 3	DISTANCE 1	Ⓡ M L	YD. LINE +41
	PLAY	T20 PASS	
	GAIN	+10	

*hit left end
hook
1st down*

DOWN	DISTANCE	R M L	YD. LINE
	PLAY		
	GAIN		

PAGE NO.

Diagram 74

begins, indicates the down, and would usually be the first down. Second column indicates yards to go, which would be ten. The third column indicates field position. The fourth column indicates side of the field laterally, right hashmark, center or left hashmark. The last column indicates the gain or loss on that particular play and is shown by a plus or minus.

Under these columns is noted the type of formation, and directly below that, the play that was run. The play is identified by a corresponding play number in our own offense. In the individual play box, the play is drawn. As soon as the play is completed, the scout would go to the next column on the right and fill in the remaining boxes prior to the running of the next play, then the third on the left and the fourth on the right.

If we look at the first play run in this particular ball game, we will see that when play was initiated it was first and ten on the opponent's 45-yard line on the left side of the field. The play was run from a full house or straight T backfield, and it was a power sweep, which we call in our offense play #20, and it netted a gain of four yards. If we look at the adjoining column, we can see that it is now second down and six yards to go. Field position is the middle of the field, and the formation was a full house or straight T backfield. The play run was a 38 or full-back up the middle in our offense. It netted eight yards, but a fumble occurred and the opponents recovered. Because the ball changed hands, boxes three and four were not used on this series.

Now, looking at the next page, we see the next series of downs when the team being scouted again had possession of the ball. Looking at the first column, we can see that they took possession first and ten on the 50-yard line, on the left hashmark. The play run was from a full house backfield (play #22) for a four-yard gain. Looking at the adjoining box, it is now second down and six yards to go on the opponent's 46-yard line, in the middle of the field. The formation is a full house backfield, and the play run is a 46 dive for a five-yard gain. On the bottom box the down is third, the distance is one yard on the opponent's 40-yard line, formation a full house, and the play a 20 pass (a running pass by the left halfback) for a ten-yard gain. Because they made the first down, the page would be flipped and there would be nothing in the fourth box. If they did not make the first down and the ball was punted, in the fourth box would be written "punted," the yardage of the punt, and the punt formation drawn.

TENDENCY CHART

The second chart we use is our tendency chart (Diagram 75). From the individual play charts, we transfer the individual plays to our tendency chart. This is done one at a time from the first play to the last play of the game. The first column is for the numbers of each play run during the game listed chronologically. The second column has to do with the down; third column with distance for the down; and the fourth column is the field position indicated by a minus or plus sign; i.e., if the team had the ball on their own 30-yard line, it would be indicated by +20. The fifth column, labeled field, indicates in what position laterally the ball is located, left hashmark, middle or right hashmark. The sixth column indicates the formation used on that particular play. The seventh column indicates the play run, and this is described by the terms and numbering system of our own offensive formation. The eighth column has to do with the gain on the play, indicated by plus or minus the number of yards, or left blank if no gain. The last column headed "Comments" is used for any additional information pertinent to a particular play that might be of value.

The following tendency chart used in a specific game illustrates the information required by the scout.

NO.	DOWN	DISTANCE	FIELD POSITION	FIELD	FORMATION	PLAY	GAIN	COMMENT
1	1	10	−36		WL PR	45	+1	DRIVE
2	2	9	−37		WR PL	24	+8	DRIVE
3	3	1	−45		WL PR	45	+7	DRIVE
4	1	10	48		WL PR SER	45	−1	
5	2	11	49		WR PL	24	+6	
6	3	5	43		WR PL	24	+12	
7	1	10	31		SLOT RT. PL	PASS	+11	SPRINT OUT RT.
8	1	10	20		WL PL	27	+1	WEDGE
9	2	9	19		WL PL	38	+1	WEDGE
10	3	8	18		WL PR	45	+3	
11	4	5	15		WL SER	SNEAK	+5	
12	1	10	10		DW	38	+1	
13	2	9	9		WR PR	SNEAK	+2	
14	3	7	7		WL PR	45	TD	
15	EXTRA PT.				KICK			GOOD
16	1	10	26		WL PR	34	+4	OFF FAKE 46
17	2	6	20		WL PR	30	−1	PITCH
18	3	7	21		WL PR	45	−1	
19	4	8	22		FIELD GOAL			BLOCKED

COMMACK

Diagram 75

NO.	DOWN	DISTANCE	FIELD POSITION	FIELD	FORMATION	PLAY	GAIN	COMMENT
20	1	10	-40		WR PL	24	+2	DRIVE
21	2	8	-42		WR PL	41 REV.	-20	DEVELOPED SLOW-DEEP
22	3	28	-22		WR PL	PASS	-1	RUSH
23	4	29	-21		KICK			44 YDS.
24	1	10	-44		WR PL	24	+5	
25	2	5	-49		WL PL	49	+8	OFF FAKE 36
26	1	10	43		WR PL	39	+2	WEDGE
27	2	8	41		WR PR	44 DELAY	+2	WING BLOCKS IN
28	3	6	39		WL PR	34	+12	OFF FAKE 46
29	1	10	27		WR PL	PASS	INC.	WING OVER MIDDLE
30	2	10	-48		WL PR	38	+1	
31	3	9	-49		WR PL	20	+10	PITCH
32	1	10	41		WL PR	45	+3	
33	2	7	38		WL PL	22	+5	DRIVE
34	3	2	33		DW	38	+3	
35	1	10	30		DW	33	-2	
36	2	12	32		WL PL	22	+11	
37	1	10	21		WR PR	38	+1	
38	2	9	20		WL PR	PASS	-3	RUSH

COMMACK

Diagram 75 (cont'd.)

NO.	DOWN	DISTANCE	FIELD POSITION	FIELD	FORMATION	PLAY	GAIN	COMMENT
39	3	12	23		WL PL	PASS	−1	RUSH
40	4	13	24		WR PL	PASS	INC.	LEFT END FLY
			HALF	7-6	W. I.			
41	1	10	−36		WR PR	45	+2	DRIVE
42	2	8	−38		WR PR	10	+4	POWER
43	3	4	−42		WR PL	35	0	DRIVE
44	4	4	−42		KICK			37 YD.
45	1	10	−28		WR PR SEL	30	+7	PITCH
46	2	3	−35		WR PR	45	+2	DRIVE
47	3	1	−37		WR PL	24	+1	
48	1	10	−38		WR PL	PASS	INC.	WING SIDELINE
49	2	10	−38		WR PR	45	+2	
50	3	8	−40		WR PL	PASS	+9	WING SIDE LINE-10 YD.
51	1	10	−49		WL PR	45	0	
52	2	10	−49		WR PR	45	+2	
53	3	8	49		WR PR	10	−2	
54	4	10	−49		KICK	PEN. ROUGHING		
55	1	10	44		WL PL	24	+18	
56	1	10	26		WR PL	PASS	+4	LEFT END BUTTON
				COMMACK				

Diagram 75 (cont'd.)

NO.	DOWN	DISTANCE	FIELD POSITION	FIELD	FORMATION	PLAY	GAIN	COMMENT
57	2	6	22		WR PL	PASS	INC.	WING DEEP
58	3	6	22		WR PL	FUMBLE		
59	1	10	-39		WR PR	45	+4	
60	2	6	-43		WL PL	SNEAK	+2	
61	3	4	-45		WL PL	38	+2	
62	4	2	-47		WR PR	45	+6	
63	1	10	47		WL PR	PASS	-6	RUSH
64	2	16	-47		WL PL	PASS	+4	SPRINT OUT LEFT
65	3	12	49		WR PR	PASS	INC.	SPRINT OUT RT.
66	4	12	49		WR PR	SCREEN PASS	+17	WING COMES LEFT
			18-7 COMMACK					
			COMMACK					

Diagram 75 (cont'd.)

Diagram 76

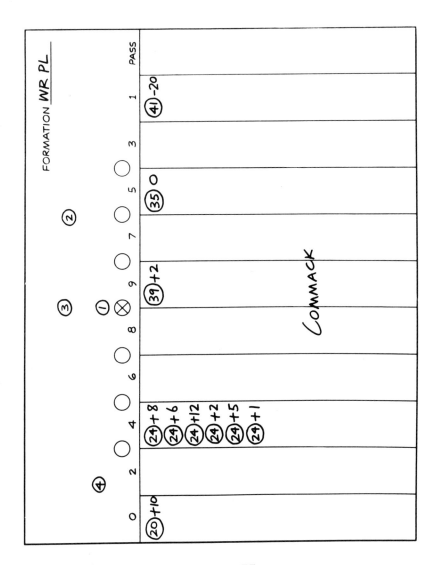

Diagram 77

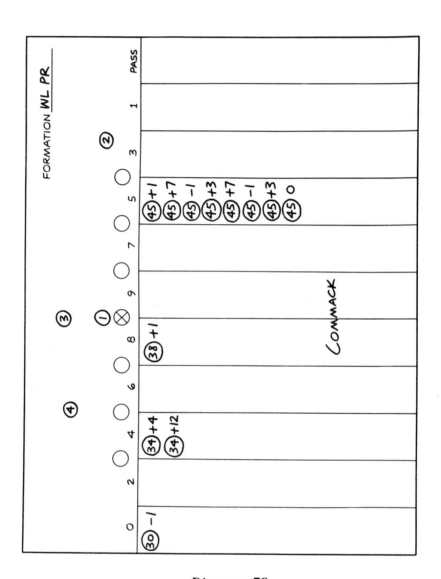

Diagram 78

The illustration shows how the information gathered by the scout is compiled into the tendency chart. This is done for two or three games. We can now tell in what sequence a play may be called, and the situation in the game which requires that particular play.

From the tendency chart, we will transfer each individual play to our formation chart (Diagram 76). The offense is on top, and we draw in the formation from which the play was run. If the scouted team ran out of three formations, we would have three formation charts, or if they ran out of seven formations, we would have seven charts. For each formation the scouted team uses we have one chart. The formation will be labeled on top, and the backfield drawn in.

FORMATION CHART

Then from the tendency chart, we will transfer the plays in chronological order to the formation chart. When completed, it will look as it does in Diagrams 77 and 78. Each individual formation chart will have every play run from that formation, the number of times run, and the gain. It will also contain the pass plays thrown in this formation.

In each formation chart we want each individual play listed in this chart drawn and stapled to it, including pass patterns. From this, we can look at the formation chart, see which particular play was run the most and for what yardage, and see exactly how the play was run on the attached page.

To summarize our scouting report:

1. *Individual play chart*—This is our work-play sheet with four plays per sheet used at the game itself.
2. *Tendency chart*—Each individual play is transferred to the tendency chart from the play chart. This chart is used to determine which particular plays will be called in different situations throughout the game. With three games of tendency charts, we can analyze and predict fairly accurately a play in specific situation.

WL PR (45)

WR PL (24)

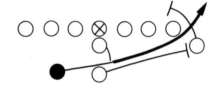

WL PR (30)

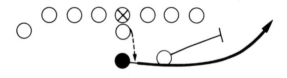

Diagram 79

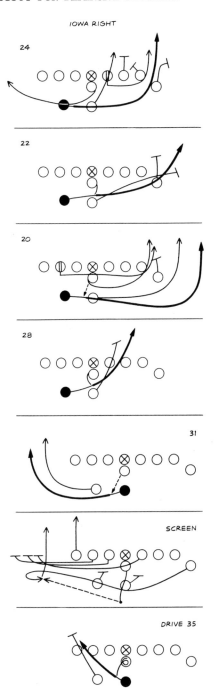

Diagram 80

3. *Formation charts*—From the tendency chart we transfer all plays to the specific formation chart. From this, we can tell from what formation each play was run, with what consistency, and which plays were most successful and must be stopped. It will also give us an idea of which back carries the ball most often and from what formation.

4. *Individual plays*—From the formation chart, the scout will draw the individual plays including pass patterns (Diagrams 79-80). These are used to determine exactly how each type of play is run, and as a guide for our foreign team coach in running against the varsity defense in practice.

THE KICKING GAME

The kicking game is scouted by answering the questions and drawing the formations as seen on page 167.

PERSONNEL

Before the scouted game begins, the scout purchases a program and circles the names of the offensive and defensive starters. Although we are primarily concerned with formations and tendencies, we do try to determine any individual characteristics of particular ball players. Our scout is concentrating on each specific play and normally has little time to pick out individual player tendencies. When he does find an unusual or outstanding characteristic of a ball player, he will note it on the work sheet, and then further note it in his summary. We do want individual players' names, weights and sizes (probably from the program), and from this we make a chart and place it in the football team room.

At the conclusion of the scouting report, we ask the scout to write a summary of his opinion of the team scouted. It should include the type of ball team, and its personality; for example: aggressive, polished, awkward, disciplined, determined, lackadaisical, poorly conditioned, big, championship calibre, green, unsure, disheartened, spirited, experienced, etc.

13

HOW TO DEVELOP
A WEIGHT TRAINING PROGRAM
FOR A WINNING DEFENSE

It is of the utmost importance to develop the high school athlete in his sophomore or junior year through a progressive weight training program. At Northport the coaching staff sets up such a program in the off season, working throughout the winter and spring. We encourage all boys interested in playing Northport Varsity football the next fall to participate in the program. We are looking for "bulk growth" in weight, size and strength. Progressive exercise with barbells is a quick, safe and effective way of developing muscle and body strength. In order for muscles to become stronger and larger it is necessary for them to contract against resistance that is gradually increased. It is also essential that each muscle group in the body be given an amount of resistance appropriate to its particular strength.

I am of the firm belief that there are no disadvantages or legitimate objections to modern scientific weight training. Some believe that weight training makes the individual slow, stiff jointed and without mobility. These ideas are, I believe, hangovers from ignorance and old superstitions. Our coaching staff wholeheartedly endorses a sound weight training program for all boys participating in varsity athletics.

FIVE EXERCISES FOR OUR PROGRAM

We have selected five exercises which serve as a basis for our program. These are: military press, bench press, reverse curls, pullovers and curls. I have indicated here the correct way to perform these exercises as we do them at Northport.

Military Press

Clear the weight to the shoulders, and with moderate slowness push the bar upward until the arms are completely straight. Then lower the bar to the shoulders, not to the floor, and repeat the press. The body must be erect, and the arms straightened fully each time and lowered to the chest. Inhale as the bar is raised, and exhale as the bar is lowered. The military press is for the strengthening of the upper arm muscles.

Bench Press

Begin by lying on a narrow bench, legs hanging on the side and feet flat on the floor. Raise bar from chest upward until arms are straight up, and slowly lower it again to the chest. This exercise is for strengthening of the chest and upper arm muscles.

Reverse Curl

Stand erect, feet apart, holding bar across thighs using over-grip. The arms should be straight with the wrists bent upward. Raise the bar slowly all the way to the shoulders. The hands should be kept bent upward at the wrist throughout the movement, and the elbows must remain stationary and close to the sides of the body. The body must be kept erect, not bent backward.

Curl

Stand erect, feet apart, holding bar across thighs using an under-grip. The arms should be straight with the wrists bent upward. Raise bar slowly until arms are completely bent. Body must be kept erect, elbows stationary. Lower bar to first position slowly. Both the curl and the reverse curl are excellent for strengthening biceps and forearm muscles.

Pullover

Position similar to the bench press except that head extends over the end of the bench downward. Grasp bar on the floor with under-grip, and raise it over the head to the chest. Then slowly lower it back to first position. Inhale as bar is raised; exhale as bar is lowered.

To begin our weight training program, we call a meeting near the end of January for all football candidates intending to turn out the following season. We detail the purpose, function and organization of the program at this time, and explain that it is a prerequisite to the next football season.

All participants are encouraged to work out with the weights three times every week. A workout consists of the five exercises listed in this chapter performed in three sets. Each exercise is repeated ten times per set. A typical workout, then, would consist of each exercise performed approximately 30 times, or three sets of ten with a pause of several minutes between sets. Each boy will experiment with the proper weight on the bar for each exercise until he finds a starting weight to work from. We tell the boy that the proper weight to begin with should be determined by finding the weight with which he could not finish the third set of exercises. For example: if a boy was using 140 pound bench press, he should be capable of pressing 140 pounds the first two sets, but not able to press the full ten exercises of the third set. When he is capable of lifting the total weight all 30 times, or completing three sets, he must add ten pounds to his bar for that particular exercise on his next workout.

WORKOUT PROGRESS CHART

Each boy is responsible for planning the time available to him for workouts. The staff does not set up a schedule of workouts for participants to follow. It is up to each individual to put forth as much or as little effort as he sees fit. We have, however, made workouts quick and easy for the boys by welding the weights on to the bar. The bars are weighted from 70 pounds on up to 230 pounds, with 10 pound graduates. This facilitates quick use of weights for spare time workouts, lunch periods, free periods or before or after school. It is also an effective way of keeping track of the weights.

At the preliminary meeting each candidate is given a card (Figure 1), and we record each boy's weight and height on his card. Times are set for subsequent meetings to demonstrate the correct performance of each exercise by the coaching staff. At the end of the week each boy will have ascertained his correct beginning weight for each exercise. After each workout the boy is to circle the date of the workout on the back of his card (Figure 2).

This enables the staff to check at a glance the number of workouts the boy has had.

We like to motivate the boys and to "keep them honest" by testing them about once each month. We call all candidates together after school and test them on one of the five exercises, without their knowing which one. Each boy is given two opportunities to perform the exercise, pressing the most weight he can. We record the maximum weight on his card, and from that we make a master list. Those pressing the most weight are put at the top of the list, and those pressing the least at the bottom. Thus we have a progress report of each participant on a month-to-month basis. This, of course, stimulates healthy competition among the boys and keeps the interest level high at all times. From the individual cards we can see the progress made, and know when a particular boy needs encouragement in weight gain, or another in weight loss but increased strength.

Figure 3 is the completed chart of one boy participating in the program.

Name _____ Year _____ Position _____

Address _____ Phone _____

	Height	Weight	Mil. Press	Bench Pr.	Rev. Curl	Pull Over	Curl
Feb. 1							
Mar. 1							
Apr. 1							
May 1							
June 1							
Sept. 1							

Figure 1

FEB ⑦ 8 ⑨ 12 13 ⑭ 15 ⑳ ㉓ 26 ㉗ 28 ㉙

MARCH 3 4 ⑤⑥⑦ 8 9 10⑪ 12 13 14 15 16 17⑱ 19 20 21㉒ 23 24 ㉕ 26㉗ 28 29 30 31

APRIL ①②③ 4 5 6 7 8 9 10⑪ 12 13 14 15 ⑯ 17 18 19 20 21㉒ 23 24 ㉕ 26 27 28 ㉙ 30

MAY ① 2 3 4 5 6 7 8 9 ⑩ 11 12 ⑬ 14 15 ⑯⑰ 18 19 ⑳㉑ 22㉓ 24 25 26 27㉘ 29 ㉚ 31

JUNE ① 2 3 4 ⑤⑥ 7 8 9 ⑩ 11 ⑫ 13 ⑭ 15 ⑯ 17 18 19 20 21 22 23 24 25 26 27

Figure 2

BENCH PRESS (200) (230) (240) (250)

MIL. PRESS (170) (190)

CURL (120) (150)

Name PHIL ROSE

Address 7 ASHLAND PLACE E.N.P.

Year 10th Position LINE

Phone AN 1 - 2028

	Height	Weight	Mil. Press	Bench Pr.	Rev. Curl	Pull Over	Curl
Feb. 1	68½	168	85	125	75	65	75
Mar. 1	69	177	95	140	85	85	90
Apr. 1	69	184	105	155	95	105	100
May 1	69	187	135	175	110	135	115
June 1	69½	189	145	195	120	155	115
Sept.1	70	195	155	220	130	170	125

Figure 3

You can see the unusual growth made from month to month by this particular boy. On February 1 he weighed in at 168 pounds, and six months later on September 1 he weighed 195 pounds and was almost two inches taller. On the top of the card the numbers circled indicate the weight pressed on particular test days. On the left we see four tests of the bench press and the monthly progress. On the first test he was able to press 200 pounds, and the last time tested he could then press 250 pounds. To the right are shown two tests of the military press indicating an increase of 20 pounds. The third column lists two tests on curls showing an increase of 30 pounds. This is an impressive growth, though not unusual in our program.

We try not to exert pressure on the boys during this program, with the exception of tests each month. Then we make it constructive pressure, encouraging progress and motivating with praise where indicated.

This entire weight training program is an effective, easily organized method of improving the body growth, strength and conditioning of our football candidates. It is an excellent way of getting to know the boys and to recognize how conscientiously each may participate. The program has greatly improved our total football picture at Northport High School.

14

ELEVEN INGREDIENTS FOR WINNING ON DEFENSE

To win on any high school level of football, you must have the following ingredients:

1. You must want to win. Winning must become extremely important to all members of the team and coaching staff. If there is not a strong desire to win on the part of *all* concerned with your football team; if only one person drags his feet; if there is not enough devotion to work as hard as necessary to produce a winner; you will not have that will to win, and without that will to win, you can never be more than mediocre.

2. You must have reasons for winning. Each boy must have a reason in his own mind for wanting desperately to win. The reasons vary with each individual on a football squad. They vary from pride in school and community; to great tradition; to tangible means of advancement for the individual (such as college athletic scholarships). Reasons could involve recognition for the individual or the team as a whole; a means of expressing emotions or of distinguishing oneself from the average—whatever the reasons may be, each individual and the team as a whole must have definite motivations for winning.

3. You must sacrifice to win. Without great sacrifice, the dynamic tension and effort that come with an important football game would not be evident. Winning football demands sacrifice by each member of the squad and the coaching staff. You must give up something to obtain something else. We like to tell our football team each day that they must sacrifice something every day of the year for football. Without great sacrifice, no team ever rises to the top.

4. Be willing to work harder than anyone else. A winning football team must be well indoctrinated with the idea that they must work harder than anyone else to continue to win. We explain to our team over and over again that we continue to win not because of great athletes or coaching, but because we are willing to work harder than any other team that we play. We all must push ourselves beyond our means so that we know we have worked harder than our opponents when we go into a ball game. We know that if we work harder, victory will mean more to us than it would to our opponents. The harder you have worked, the more difficult it is to surrender.

5. Have a set plan. Once your varsity squad has this tremendous desire to win, and is willing to sacrifice and to work harder than anyone else, there must be an overall plan for victory. This plan is based on the long range goals set up during an entire season and started the preceding year in preparation for the coming campaign. It must be a master plan which incorporates each ball game into an entire season and constitutes the overall team philosophy, stating what will be emphasized, and just what are the goals set for each game within the entire season. These goals must become established and made known to the entire team.

For example: The overall plan may include the goal of allowing the opponents an average of no more than seven points per game. This of course is a defensive attitude and part of a total defensive philosophy. Another such goal is that the team must average over 250 yards per game on the ground. Then, when all the goals are established, there must be a set procedure for attaining each goal in the total season plan. Without a set plan, and without goals and ways of attaining each goal in the set plan, it will become difficult to win consistently. Each game is an entity in itself, but must be part of a total plan for the entire season.

6. Maintain great pressure. Football is a game of contact and mental determination. For football players to perform their best under stress in game situations, they must become accustomed to great pressure. We feel that if an athlete is to play beyond his capabilities, he must be pushed to the greatest extent possible. In order to do this, the entire environment surrounding the total football program must always be burdened with tense mental pressure. At no time do we want to reduce pressure. We will constantly build pressure from day to day and from week to week throughout the football season.

7. Accept nothing but perfection. In order to win consistently, you must constantly work on perfecting everything that you do. Everything that must be taught must be broken down into small parts and drilled until perfection is accomplished. As a coaching staff, you must accept nothing less than perfection. Because this is almost an impossibility, you must constantly work with your athletes to reach for perfection. Under no circumstances should you ever be satisfied with any portion of the total football program until a victory is won, and then this satisfaction should last only briefly in preparation for next victory. Never be satisfied.

8. Have all athletes work to peak performance. All your athletes must be pushed to the highest degree to reach their maximum potential. Unless this is accomplished, it is impossible to win consistently. This must be done by prodding, pushing, encouraging, motivating, evaluating, and by having each ball player relinquish his own identity into that of the entire team. The successful coaches I have watched through the years have had the ability to take average ball players and push them to their highest peak, and make them play better than the talent that they possess. To have athletes reach this peak performance, they must be pushed to the edge of complete physical endurance. I believe this is simply illustrated by looking at all the track records which are broken. It is always under extreme pressure in meet competition that a boy will reach his highest degree of performance. Under a combination of extreme pressure and hard work, good athletes can become great ones.

9. Have constant evaluation. Evaluation must be continual. Each day's practice must be evaluated and each day's accomplishments and goals determined. Every game film must be dissected and graded and evaluated. Normal progression requires that each segment of the total set plan must be evaluated. Without evaluation, a laziness develops among staff and players. And, of course, the simplest means of complete evaluation is to look back over the past season and count your victories. That is your ultimate barometer. It never lies!

10. Play the winners. You've got to play the team members who want to win very badly regardless of size, speed or ability. These are the ones who, over a period of time, will give you a consistent edge. Play the winners! What does that really mean? I like to look for the winner several different ways. The first ingredient is that he wants to win at everything, whether it be checkers, races, cards, or competition for grades. He is never satisfied unless he is winning. It depresses him to lose. He is elated whenever he wins at anything. There is a driving intensity toward competition of any kind. He is the type of individual who worries about losing and worries so deeply that it drives him to win. When you find this type of boy, no matter what his size or speed, shuffle your personnel around and get him into the lineup. If you've got two or three of these boys around, you're in for a good season! He will do the things that are not in the book, and cannot be coached for. Don't worry about his ability. Close your eyes and play the winners.

11. Talk to them every day. Make them believe they are going to win and they will.

Recently, Northport High School was carrying a 16 game undefeated streak going into the sixth game of the season.

This streak, extending over a three-year period, became a weighty burden on the team and coaching staff. Although not generally superstitious, the staff had worn the same clothing on game days for the win streak period. On one occasion, our line coach, Tom DiNuovo, had forgotten to wear a tie clip he had worn throughout the streak. Upon discovering this, he called his wife to have her bring the clip to him. She arrived just before game time and sent in the clip. Tom was so greatly relieved to have the tie clip on that all the pressure of the game seemed to drain from him. He was filled with assurance that we were going to win because the absence of the tie clip had been remedied!

When our 16 game winning streak came to an end, we felt a relief, an almost miserable relief! We were a strong favorite to win the game, and we were overconfident. We went down to a 33–0 stunning defeat. It was the next to the last game of the season and to win the championship we had to win our final game. This crushing defeat jolted us into reality, and we set about the task of working tediously on fundamentals to prepare our team for the final game and the championship. The prevailing attitude was determination. The aura of invincibility was gone.

Our worthy opponent was one of the strongest and toughest teams in the country. The tension was unbearable. On the morning of the game our backfield coach, Billy Martin, was about to leave his home, when his wife noted that he was not wearing the usual blue shirt, and commented on it. Billy icily stared at her, and in a tense monotone replied, "Blue shirts don't win football games; knocking people down wins football games!" *That's the secret I've learned in ten years of coaching.*

INDEX